MANAGER II: A Simulation

MANAGER II: A SIMULATION

Jerald R. Smith

University of Louisville

Houghton Mifflin Company   Boston

Dallas   Geneva, Illinois   Lawrenceville, New Jersey   Palo Alto

Cover Photo: Martin Paul

Printed in the U.S.A.

ISBN: 0-395-40030-9

ABCDEFGHIJ-A-898765

CONTENTS

PREFACE

MANAGER: A Simulation is a business game designed for students enrolled in an introductory management course. It provides student players with simulated real-world experience in managerial decision making, and enables them to see the relevance of the principles being taught in the course. Unlike other business games, *MANAGER: A Simulation* is simple enough to learn in a fifty-minute period and yet includes all of the variables a student needs to know in order to understand the major concepts of the introductory course. An additional benefit for players of *MANAGER: A Simulation* is that they will experience early in their education how the various functional areas of business mesh together and affect each other.

In playing the game, students acting as management teams make a variety of decisions that will have an impact on their company's operations. The decisions that each team must make include: price of the product, total marketing expense, production level, production engineering budget, research and development, size of production facilities, dividends, and capital procurement. A unique and optional feature of *MANAGER: A Simulation* is the inclusion of social responsibility and business ethic incidents that the firm faces in each decision period. Student decisions are recorded on Decision Forms and can be quickly analyzed and evaluated by a microcomputer. The instructor needs no computer knowledge to administer the game.

The objectives of *MANAGER: A Simulation* are:

1. To allow students in each major academic area (marketing, management, and so on) to make decisions that cross over functional lines and to observe how, in making major organizational decisions, one must consider all aspects of the firm

2. To provide the opportunity for student interaction in organization teamwork

3. To improve the student's communication, leadership, and interpersonal relations skills

4. To develop logical and rational decision making

5. To demonstrate the importance of such management tools as budgeting, forecasting, and long-range planning

6. To introduce the student to various ethical — or business responsibility — problems that might occur in a firm and to show the consequences of the decisions that are made

The game administrator is provided with an Instructor's Manual that explains how to play the game and provides suggestions for grading the performance of student teams and a floppy disk that analyzes and evaluates student decisions.

Unfortunately, no business simulation duplicates real life. This simulation, however, attempts to build a game model that is as close as possible to actual conditions. It is hoped that student teams will approach the gaming process as a challenge to use their knowledge to operate a business successfully. Your suggestions for improving *MANAGER: A Simulation* will be sincerely appreciated.

ACKNOWLEDGMENTS

To the late Professor Emeritus William McGlothlin who taught me that one learns best by doing. To my father who taught me many practical elements of business and to my mother who taught me what business ethics means.

To my many colleagues in the Association of Business Simulation and Experiential Learning whose annual meetings have been a constant source of help and inspiration.

To Jane Goldstein and her talented staff at the University of Louisville School of Business for their patience in teaching me what word processing is all about.

To my family for their unrelenting support: Carolyn, Susan, David, Flossie, and Annetta.

1

THE HISTORY AND BACKGROUND

The Industry

The firm your team will be operating is one of several in the automobile radio industry. All are relatively small firms with annual sales of $3.5 to $4 million. Each of the competing firms is relatively new and has had modest profits in the past. Each is marketing an FM/AM auto radio which is not part of the original auto equipment; the radio is installed by the owner or by a radio shop for the owner. Most of the firms in the industry sell through wholesalers, discount houses, and auto radio shops. The manufacturers have kept the wholesale price fairly close to $40, and the radio retails for $65 - $100. There are firms that produce a much higher priced radio ($100 - $350 retail), but these are not your competition; your competitors are all producing a relatively low-priced product.

The total market potential is affected by (1) general economic conditions, (2) the total marketing expenditure, (3) research and development expenditure, and (4) pricing decisions. The potential share of the market for each firm is a function of the relationship of its decisions to those of its competitors.

The Company

The company your management team is taking over has been in business only one year and has been making modest profits. The current president wishes to pursue other business interests and has hired your management team to assume management of the firm. The company is short on working capital and is operating close to its production capacity. Thus, the first major decisions by your team will involve capital procurement and enlargement of the manufacturing facility.

Maximization of profit is a key objective of the game, but other objectives are of importance also. These include:

1. Maintaining a prudent cash position
2. Keeping a reasonable inventory on hand
3. Maintaining a fair share of the market
4. Utilizing plant capacity
5. Being a good citizen in the community
6. Keeping the price of the common stock at reasonable levels

PAST OPERATING CHARTS

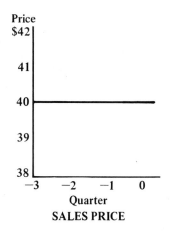

SALES PRICE

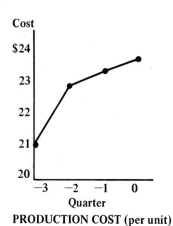

PRODUCTION COST (per unit)

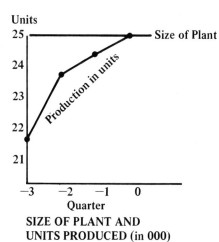

SIZE OF PLANT AND
UNITS PRODUCED (in 000)

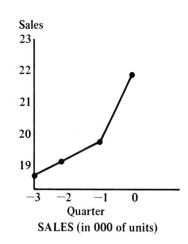

SALES (in 000 of units)

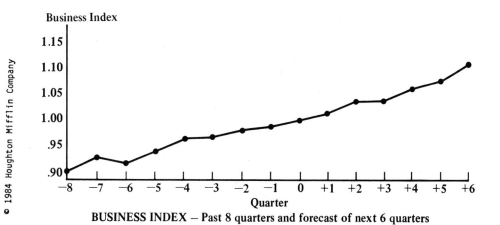

BUSINESS INDEX – Past 8 quarters and forecast of next 6 quarters

2

THE ENVIRONMENT
AND PROCESS

Decision Information

PRODUCTION MANAGEMENT

Size of Plant

The plant currently has the capacity to produce 24,250 radios per quarter. Additional capacity can be obtained by investing $40 per additional unit desired in "Plant Addition" on the decision form. *Construction of additional capacity takes one quarter.* (See Depreciation, below.)

Scheduling

Teams should use all forecasting methods obtainable in order to accurately predict sales and the corresponding production to support sales. Selling out of the product (a "stock-out") is just as undesirable as accumulating excess inventory. If the firm cannot meet all its orders in a period, those unfilled orders do *not* carry over to the next period, but go to a competitor in the *same* period. Each unsold unit that must be held in inventory costs approximately $1 for storage expenses. Minimum inventory cost each period is $1,000. Inventory costing is on the "last in, first–out" system. This means that goods carried over from one period to the next are carried on the books at their most current cost.

Production Engineering

Expenditures in this category will support the firm's production engineering department in improving production line efficiency through time and motion studies, more efficient equipment layout, and other cost-saving programs. The major benefit is in decreasing variable production costs. The major effect of additional budgeting in this area will take place the upcoming quarter. Last quarter the firm budgeted $10,000 for this department.

Cost Characteristics

Production costs will increase as plant utilization nears 100 percent capacity as well as when utilization is less than the optimum. Thus, overtime, increased maintenance, and decreased efficiency of peak capacity will raise the unit cost of a product. The additional apportionment of fixed costs to a smaller number of units will also make the unit cost higher than if the plant is operating at the optimum level. One could expect that a plant of this type would have an optimum (cost) level when production is at a level of from 70 to 90% of capacity. Last quarter the firm produced 25,000 units (maximum capacity), and the per-unit cost was $23.52.

DEPRECIATION

Depreciation of plant and equipment is computed at the rate of 3% per quarter. Depreciation, a noncash cost, is charged as an expense to determine taxable income but is not shown on the cash flow statement. The plant capacity will decrease by 3% per quarter unless an equal amount is expended each quarter for additional capacity. This would amount to $30,000 for the upcoming quarter (just to keep the plant capacity at its current 24,250-unit capacity). The maximum plant addition in any one quarter is $200,000 (5,000 units).

MARKETING MANAGEMENT

Pricing

The firm is currently pricing its product at $40 per unit to all customers. The freight is paid by the customer (FOB). Most of the competition has priced close to this level in the past, and very little price cutting has taken place in the industry. However, with more national discount chains carrying this type of product, sharper price competition is expected in the industry.

Marketing Expenditure

Currently, the firm is budgeting $90,000 per quarter to the marketing department. This is used to support the missionary sales force, advertising efforts, and sales promotions. Additional expenditures in marketing would have the largest effect during the quarter in which the additional amount was budgeted; however, there would be a small residual effect carried over to the next quarter.

Research and Development

Expenditures in the firm's R & D program may bring about an improved product that will be more desirable to the consumer and result in increased sales. The probability of success of any R & D program is likely to be related to the program's size, consistency, and durability. There is a point of diminishing returns in most R & D operations. The firm you are taking over has a fairly modest R & D budget of $10,000 per quarter.

Market Research

Various market research studies may be announced by the game administrator during the course of the simulation. Teams that purchase these studies will pay for them in the Other Expense block of the decision form.

FINANCIAL MANAGEMENT

Sources of Capital

The firm is currently low on working capital. There are three methods of obtaining additional funds. The first is through a bank loan. Bank loans may be made at any time during the game and may be made for a term of three months to three years. The bank would expect quarterly payments to be made on the principle; this payment should be no less than 1/12 of the original loan and should be paid quarterly. Such a payment is indicated on the decision form by using a minus sign (−) in front of the repayment under Bank Loans. Teams are expected to pay off the loan with the proper notation on the decision form without further instructions. In other words, the repayment of the loan is not automatically assumed. Teams may pay off the loan at a faster rate if desired.

Interest charges are automatically computed and charged to the expense statement and no action is required by the team. Current interest rates are 4% per quarter (16% annually). Interest rates in the future could be higher or lower than the current rate. Any changes will be announced by the instructor.

A second method of obtaining additional funds is by selling additional shares of common stock. The corporation has been authorized by its state charter to issue a total of 12,000 shares of stock. It has issued only 7,000 shares to date, so you can sell up to 5,000 additional shares. Stock is sold at the current price as shown on the printout.

The third method of obtaining additional funds is by retaining the profits as they are made. Of course, a portion of the profits ($7,000 per quarter) is currently paid out to the stockholders, and you may wish to continue this practice, decrease the amount, or increase the amount. The total accumulated profits kept by the firm for its own use are termed Retained Earnings. This account is merely an accounting entry for these funds retained by the firm in the past; the funds have been used in a variety of ways — new facilities, equipment, inventory, and so on. It does *not* represent ready cash; additional cash *may* be available the quarter in which profits were generated, but to determine this, you will need to check the Cash line of the balance sheet.

Cash Flow

The firm should make a thorough analysis of its anticipated inflow and outflow of cash using the Cash Flow Analysis form provided in Chapter 8 of this manual. If expenditures are expected to exceed cash income, then additional capital procurement will have to be made. As stated above, additional capital can be attained through (1) a bank loan, (2) the sale of additional common stock, or (3) retention of profits earned. If a firm does not plan its cash flow well and has a negative cash balance, the bank will cover the overdraft at an interest rate of 7% per quarter. This overdraft will be included with any loans outstanding under Loans Payable on the balance sheet.

Dividends

Each firm is expected to establish a dividend policy. Retention of earnings for financing company growth is a conservative and well-accepted policy. However, the stockholders' position must also be considered carefully and a policy developed that is most equitable to all parties. Currently, the firm is paying $1.00 per share per quarter in dividend ($7,000 per quarter).

Stock Price

Each quarter, the firm's common stock price will be quoted on the computer printout. The stock price is a function of the firm's sales and profits, financial condition, dividends paid, R & D expenditure, and general economic conditions. The stock price may be considered as *one* indicator of the relative standings among firms but it does not indicate long-term trends. The firm's current stock price is $108 per share.

Overhead and Fixed Expense

The firm's overhead and fixed expenses are currently $100,000 per quarter. The firm could absorb a growth of up to 50% without this expense changing. If the firm expands beyond 50%, overhead can be expected to increase

$50,000 for each 50% increment in increased production capability. Therefore, when plant size exceeds 37,500 units, overhead costs will increase to $150,000 per quarter.

Operating Statements

A copy of the firm's computer printout for the previous quarter is included in the manual. It includes an income and expense statement, cash flow analysis, abbreviated balance sheet, and unit cost, ending inventory, business index, and stock price information. In addition, information concerning the previous quarter's decision incident will be included.

QUARTERLY INCIDENTS

In addition to making operating decisions, each team will be presented with a different "incident" each period. The incident will cover some area of business ethics or social responsibility. Read the incident carefully, discuss it thoroughly within the team, and select one of the alternatives listed. Then place the number indicating your decision on the decision form. The instructor may want your team to justify your decision in writing and submit it with the decision form. (See Chapter 3 for Incident #1.)

QUARTERLY DECISIONS

Each decision period, the team should make its decisions and complete the decision form.

Form D-9:   Decision Form

QUARTER NO. _____ COMPANY NO. _____

INDUSTRY NO. _____

1. PRICE $_____.____

2. MARKETING $_____,000

3. PRODUCTION (IN UNITS)   _____,000

4. PRODUCTION ENGINEERING $_____,000

5. RESEARCH & DEVELOPMENT $_____,000

6. PLANT ADDITION (IN DOLLARS) $_____,000

7. DIVIDENDS PAID $_____,000

8. OTHER EXPENSE $_____,000

9. BANK LOAN OR REPAYMENT $_____,000

10. STOCK SOLD (IN DOLLARS) $_____,000

11. INCIDENT   _____

VERIFICATION TOTAL[1]

* * * * * * * * * * * * * * * * * * * *

[1]NOTE: ADD ALL NUMBERS FROM ITEM 1 THROUGH 11 AND PLACE TOTAL (INCLUDING INCIDENT NUMBERS AND ANY DIGITS TO THE RIGHT OF THE DECIMAL) IN THE VERIFICATION BOX. THE VERIFICATION TOTAL SHOULD BE TOTALED ALGEBRAICALLY: NEGATIVE NUMBERS SHOULD BE SUBTRACTED FROM THE TOTAL. THIS IS USED ONLY TO VERIFY THE CORRECTNESS OF THE NUMBERS AS THEY ARE TYPED INTO THE COMPUTER. PLEASE BE SURE YOUR VERIFICATION TOTAL IS CORRECT.

OTHER INSTRUCTIONS: Omit thousands (000) from the decision form. Do *not* use commas. Put a zero (0) in any item not used. A bank loan repayment is indicated by a minus sign (−) preceding the amount to be repaid. Additional plant capacity can be constructed by expending $4,000 for each 100 units desired. (Remember, $4,000 is written as *4* in the decision blank above.)

Price

Indicate in dollars using a decimal as needed (such as 40, 40.5, 38.8, and so on). Since your firm is selling wholesale, there is little advantage in "odd" pricing (for example, $39.95). From a mechanical point of view, the fewer decimal points used on the decision forms, the less likely the computer operator will make an error when inputting your decisions.

Marketing

State in thousands of dollars. Leave off the last three zeros ($90,000 would be written as 90). For ease in inputting your decisions, use even thousands; in reality, there would be negligible sales differential between expenditures of $90,000 and $90,500 per quarter.

Production

This is an order to your production manager for a definite number of units to be produced the next quarter. Again, try to keep this in thousands without the use of the last three digits (000) and decimals (24,000 units is written as 24). You may, however, input other than even thousands with the use of a decimal. Thus, a production level of 24,250 would be written as 24.25 with no zeros following; on the following Decision Form it has been rounded to 25,000.

Production Engineering

This expenditure funds the production engineering department to investigate and implement various methods of lowering production costs. Write the decision on the form in thousands ($10,000 is written as 10).

Research & Development

The research and development budget is used by that department in an attempt to develop a better and more salable product. This expenditure should be entered on the form in thousands of dollars.

Plant Addition

This blank is used for two purposes: first, to reinvest an amount equal to the current depreciation to keep the plant capacity at a constant level, and second, to increase the plant capacity. To increase the plant capacity, invest $4,000 per 100 additional units desired. Always indicate this amount in thousands of dollars.

Dividends Paid

This is the total amount of dividends to be paid in the quarter, preferably in thousands of dollars ($7,000 is written 7). Try to keep in thousands so a decimal number is not required.

Other Expense

From time to time during the simulation, you will need to use this blank upon instruction from the instructor or as directed in the computer printout. Otherwise, put a zero (0) in this blank.

Bank Loan or Repayment

This is used to borrow additional funds from the bank or to repay the bank for a loan. A minus (−) sign in front of the dollar figure represents a loan repayment being made. Always keep in thousands of dollars, omitting the last three zeros (000). Put zero in the blank if there is no change from the previous quarter. If you want to borrow additional funds as well as repay a portion of an earlier loan, simply place the *net* figure in the blank space for loans.

Stock Sold

You may sell additional stock up to the authorized 12,000 shares. Place the dollar amount of funds you wish to net in the blank, and the correct number of shares will be sold for your company. Insert in even thousands of dollars. Do *not* insert the *number* of shares you want sold but rather the *dollars* you wish to net. Stock may be recalled (repurchased) by the company by placing a minus sign (−) in front of the dollar amount that you wish to repurchase.

Incident

One version of the simulation includes the use of social responsibility and ethical problems each quarter. If your class is using this version, place the number of your team's choice each decision period in this blank. Otherwise, place a zero (0) in the blank each quarter.

14

COPY OF DECISION FORM FOR QUARTER 0

These are the decisions made by the management of the firm in the preceding quarter before your team assumed the management of the firm. Please note how the verification total was tallied, and that production was rounded up to 25,000 units.

Form D-9: Decision Form

QUARTER NO. __0__ COMPANY NO. __X__

INDUSTRY NO. __I__

1. PRICE	$ _40_ . ___
2. MARKETING	$ __90__ ,000
3. PRODUCTION (IN UNITS)	__25__ ,000
4. PRODUCTION ENGINEERING	$ __10__ ,000
5. RESEARCH & DEVELOPMENT	$ __10__ ,000
6. PLANT ADDITION (IN DOLLARS)	$ __30__ ,000
7. DIVIDENDS PAID	$ __7__ ,000
8. OTHER EXPENSE	$ __0__ ,000
9. BANK LOAN OR REPAYMENT	$ __0__ ,000
10. STOCK SOLD (IN DOLLARS)	$ __0__ ,000
11. INCIDENT	__0__
VERIFICATION TOTAL[1]	212

* * * * * * * * * * * * * * * * * * * *

[1]NOTE: ADD ALL NUMBERS FROM ITEM 1 THROUGH 11 AND PLACE TOTAL (INCLUDING INCIDENT NUMBERS AND ANY DIGITS TO THE RIGHT OF THE DECIMAL) IN THE VERIFICATION BOX. THE VERIFICATION TOTAL SHOULD BE TOTALED ALGEBRAICALLY: NEGATIVE NUMBERS SHOULD BE SUBTRACTED FROM THE TOTAL. THIS IS USED ONLY TO VERIFY THE CORRECTNESS OF THE NUMBERS AS THEY ARE TYPED INTO THE COMPUTER. PLEASE BE SURE YOUR VERIFICATION TOTAL IS CORRECT.

OTHER INSTRUCTIONS: Omit thousands (000) from the decision form. Do *not* use commas. Put a zero (0) in any item not used. A bank loan repayment is indicated by a minus sign (−) preceding the amount to be repaid. Additional plant capacity can be constructed by expending $4,000 for each 100 units desired. (Remember, $4,000 is written as *4* in the decision blank above.)

© 1984 Houghton Mifflin Company

Sample Printout for Quarter 0 - Starting Position for All Teams

COMPANY NO. 1   PERIOD NO. 0   INDUSTRY NO. 1

INCOME & EXPENSE ANALYSIS

SALES:

23062 UNITS @ $40 EACH	$ 922	

BALANCE SHEET

EXPENSES:		
COST/GOODS SOLD	542	
PRODUCTION ENGINEERING	10	
INVENTORY EXPENSE	2	
MARKETING	90	
R & D EXPENSE	10	
OTHER EXPENSES	0	
INTEREST EXPENSE	12	
OVERHEAD/FIXED EXPENSE	100	
DEPRECIATION	30	
TOTAL EXPENSES	796	
PROFIT BEFORE TAX	126	
INCOME TAX	63	
NET PROFIT AFTER TAX	63	
DIVIDENDS PAID	7	
RETAINED EARNINGS	56	

Balance Sheet:

CASH	40
INVENTORY	46
PLANT & EQUIPMENT	970
OTHER ASSETS	0
TOTAL ASSETS	1056
LOANS PAYABLE	300
OTHER LIABILITIES	0
COMMON STOCK	700
RETAINED EARNINGS	56
TOTAL LIAB & EQUITY	1056

CASH FLOW ANALYSIS

INFLOW:

		OUTFLOW:	
SALES	922	EXPENSES – DEPRECIATION	767
BANK LOAN	0	TAXES AND DIVIDENDS	70
STOCK SOLD	0	GOODS INTO/FROM INVENTORY	46
		BANK REPAYMENT	0
		PLANT ADDITION	30
TOTAL INFLOW	922	TOTAL CASH OUTFLOW	913

NET CASH FLOW   9

OTHER INFORMATION

PRODUCTION COST (PER UNIT) $23.52
PLANT CAPACITY NEXT QUARTER IS 23524 UNITS
ENDING INVENTORY (IN UNITS)   1938

CURRENT PRICE OF COMMON STOCK $108 PER SHARE
TOTAL SHARES OF COMMON STOCK ISSUED   7000

BUSINESS INDEX THIS QUARTER IS 1.00
BUSINESS INDEX FORECAST FOR NEXT QUARTER IS 1.01

Analysis of Printout for Quarter 0

In order to better understand the printout and the information thereon, locate the items that are italicized in the text on the computer printout.

INCOME AND EXPENSE ANALYSIS

This portion (on the left-hand side of the printout) will list the firm's *Sales* (23,062), current selling price ($40), and gross income ($922,000 = 23,062 x $40). The *Cost of Goods Sold* is the production cost of only those goods sold (23,062 units sold x $23.52 unit cost = $542,000), not the total production cost for the quarter.

Production Engineering ($10,000), *Marketing Expense* ($90,000), and *R & D Expense* ($10,000) are all listed according to the decisions made by management; these are all within the control of management. The *Inventory Expense* ($2,000) is approximately $1.00 per unit for each unit unsold and in inventory at the end of the quarter (1,938 units @ $1 = $1,938 rounded to $2,000). A minimum cost of $1,000 per quarter is charged for inventory handling.

The *Interest Expense* ($12,000) is calculated and charged automatically on the *Loans Payable* balance according to the following schedule: Loans — 4% per quarter; Cash overdrafts — 7% per quarter. The *Overhead/Fixed Expense* is a constant $100,000 per quarter for up to 37,500 units of plant capacity; at that point, this expense increases $50,000 for each additional 12,500 units (or fraction thereof) of plant capacity.

Depreciation ($30,000) is calculated at 3% per quarter of beginning *Plant and Equipment* valuation ($1,000,000 x .03 = $30,000). The current ending value of *Plant and Equipment* therefore is $970,000 ($1,000,000 − $30,000). *Other Expenses* are entered occasionally by the team for certain incidental, nonrecurring expenses.

Profit Before Tax is equal to Total Sales less *Total Expenses* ($922,000 − $796,000 = $126,000). The *Income Tax* of $63,000 represents a tax rate of 50% of *Profit Before Tax* and is constant throughout the simulation. *Retained Earnings* represents the amount of profits that are being kept by the firm; remember that retained earnings are an accounting entry only and this does not represent a reserve of cash. The retained profits of a firm may have been utilized in a variety of ways — additional plant or equipment, additional inventory, or additional cash.

CASH FLOW ANALYSIS

In the middle section of the printout, there is a Cash Flow Analysis. This financial information lists the firm's cash inflow and cash outflow and indicates whether there was a positive or negative cash flow. The team can use this information to plan its cash needs and borrow additional funds or sell common stock as necessary.

Sources of cash (Inflow) consist of sales, bank loans, and sale of common stock. Uses for cash (Outflow) consist of all expenses, taxes, dividends paid, repayment of bank loans, and construction of additional plant facilities. Depreciation is a noncash expense and is not included as a cash flow item. (An explanation of this is called for at this point for those who have not had accounting.) Depreciation expensing is a method of allocating a portion of a large fixed asset (such as the manufacturing plant in this simulation) to each accounting period. Therefore, in this simulation, the plant value (currently $970,000) is "depreciated" at 3% for the upcoming quarter, making the depreciation expense $29,100. Since the plant had been paid for sometime in the past, there is no cash expense at this point, but we can use the depreciation expense as a legitimate expense for income tax purposes. This is why it is listed as an expense on the Income and Expense Analysis but not as an item for which cash was needed on the Cash Flow Analysis. Each quarter the *Plant and Equipment* figure will be decreased by the amount charged as Depreciation Expense.

If more goods were produced than were sold, the excess goods are credited (at their production cost, $23.52 each) to the *Inventory* account. Conversely, if demand was more than the units produced, the excess demand will be met out of inventory to the point of complete exhaustion of goods in inventory. Thus, a positive figure after *Goods into/from Inventory* indicates goods were placed into inventory. A minus figure (−) indicates goods had to be taken from inventory.

Loan transactions are recorded under *Bank Repayment,* and cash expended for building a larger plant is listed under *Plant Addition.* The total of all the above items represents the *Total Cash Outflow* for the quarter. If the gross sales ($922,000) do not cover this amount, the balance must come from the *Cash* account, and that account is adjusted accordingly. If the cash outflow is less than cash inflow through *Sales,* the excess results in an addition to the *Cash* account.

BALANCE SHEET

An abbreviated Balance Sheet is printed on the top right side of the computer printout. A *Cash* balance of zero (0) indicates a greater outflow of cash than inflow; the bank will automatically cover this overdraft, add the appropriate amount to *Loans Payable,* and charge 7% interest quarterly (which is added to *Interest Expense*).

The *Inventory* item is the dollar value of the current inventory; total units of inventory are shown at the bottom left of the printout as *Ending Inventory.* The *Plant & Equipment* figure ($970,000) represents the net value of such after 3% depreciation for the quarter has been deducted. This figure divided by $40 will indicate the current plant capacity ($970,000 ÷ $40 = 24,250 units). The *Plant Capacity* for the upcoming quarter is also shown on the bottom left portion of the printout. *Other Assets* is used only to allow the balance sheet to balance due to the rounding of all numbers into even thousands. The computer does "save" these small differences, and your firm will be credited with the next even thousand dollars when that is accumulated. The *Total Assets* figure is just that. As a matter of accounting principle, the total assets must equal the total liabilities plus stockholders' equity (as explained below).

The liability and owners' equity part of the balance sheet is shown next. *Loans Payable* is an indication of the total loans the firm has made. *Other Liabilities* is used to accumulate small differences due to rounding for printing out the numbers in even thousands (the same as the use of *Other Assets* in the asset portion of the balance sheet). The owners' (stockholders') equity is shown next. This consists of two items. *Common Stock* represents the amount of stock that has been sold to date. When you take over this firm, 7,000 shares have been sold for a beginning capital of $700,000. You may sell at any time any amount (in even thousands of dollars) up to the total number of shares authorized by the corporate charter (12,000); this would be an additional 5,000 shares. Stock is sold at the current market price as listed on your printout.

The second part of the owners' equity in the firm is listed as *Retained Earnings.* This part is an accumulation of all past profits less dividends paid. It represents the profits that have not been paid out to stockholders but have been retained by the firm for capital needs.

Total Liabilities and Equity is the total of this portion of the balance sheet, and this figure must equal *Total Assets.*

OTHER INFORMATION

Data of interest to the management of the firm is listed at the bottom portion of the printout. The current cost of producing the product on a per-unit basis is listed as *Production Cost*. You will want to monitor this figure closely in order to keep your costs competitive with other firms. The *Plant Capacity* is listed next. This is the maximum number of units that your firm can produce the following quarter. The inventory of unsold units at the end of the quarter is shown as *Ending Inventory*. Thus, these units are available for sale the following quarter along with the units you produce.

The *Current Price of Common Stock* is shown as well as the *Total Shares of Common Stock Issued*. The final items in this section indicate the *Business Index* for the current quarter and a *Forecast* for the upcoming quarter. The Business Index for the simulation begins at an arbitrary base-line figure of 1.00. Any changes in this number relate to the general health of the economy and will have a direct bearing on the total demand for your product. For example, if the Business Index forecast for the next period is 1.01, this would indicate the overall economic index had increased by 1%. Conversely, an index of .96 would indicate that economic conditions had decreased approximately 4% from the original starting quarter.

INDUSTRY NEWS MESSAGE

In this section, you will receive either pertinent information concerning your industry or instructional information from your instructor.

If the incident version of the simulation is being used, relevant information concerning your decision will be printed on the lower portion of the printout.

Aids for Team Organization and Decision Making

ORGANIZATION

It is recommended that each team prepare an organization chart depicting at least one level below the vice-presidential level. A team may organize itself in any manner it feels best. The following is offered as one alternative:

One Person

1. You do it all!

Two Persons

1. Chairman of the board and financial officer
2. President, responsible for marketing and production

Three Persons

1. President and treasurer
2. Vice president of marketing
3. Vice president of production

Four Persons

1. President
2. Vice president of marketing
3. Vice president of production
4. Vice president of finance

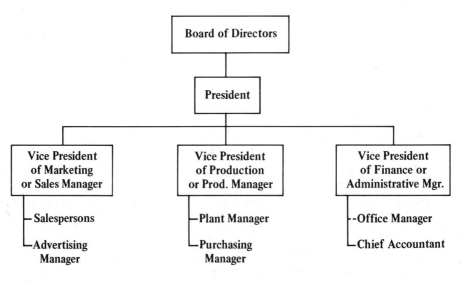

When teams are considering the best method of organizing human and financial resources, they will need to debate such topics as where the personnel management, R & D, and order department functions should be located.

ESTABLISHING PURPOSE, OBJECTIVES, AND PLANS

Purpose

The establishment of a purpose, or mission, for the firm is the first step in the strategic planning process. This short statement denotes what the organization should be doing and why it exists. It specifies exactly what the organization's business is or will be and the kind of organization it is or will be.

An example might be: "To produce and market an inexpensive automobile radio." But the question might be posed, is this mission too narrow? What happens if an opportunity arises to diversify into other related (or non-related) areas? Can your team devise a purpose, or mission, that allows for future flexibility but at the same time is not too broad?

Objectives

Objectives specify the action commitments that are being made to achieve an organization's purpose and the long-range results the management of the organization wishes to achieve. Objectives give an organization purpose and provide management with the direction needed for effective coordination of its resources. Objectives can also serve to motivate those in the organization and provide a basis for the control process in a firm.

Each team should establish its objectives as a firm. Your instructor may want these objectives written. Objectives could be established for the following areas:

1. Innovation
2. Market (or Industry) standing
3. Financial resources
4. Physical resources
5. Profitability
6. Management development
7. Personnel relations
8. Productivity
9. Social responsibility

© 1984 Houghton Mifflin Company

Plans

Merely establishing objectives, however, falls far short of completing the planning task in this area. The management team must establish plans to accomplish the desired objectives. These plans have different names in different organizations, including "action plans," "strategy," "tactical plans," and so on. For the purposes of this simulation, the term *action plan* will be used. A guide for helping the team establish its mission, objectives, and action plans is included in Chapter 7.

POLICY

After the team has established the general direction the firm should take (in the objectives), specific day-to-day guidelines must be prepared in the form of policy. Policies provide for integration of organizational goals, plans, and programs and must reflect the company's objectives. Policies should give guidance to daily activities and yet be flexible enough to allow the manager some latitude in decision making. Some of the areas for which policies may be established are:

1. Marketing policy
2. Financial policy
3. Production and purchasing policy
4. Personnel policy
5. Public relations policy
6. Innovation policy
7. Administrative policy

An example in this simulation of a policy that would aid in the decision process would be a policy concerning marketing expenditures. The team may want to establish a policy such as: "The marketing budget will be 10% of the past quarter's sales" (or 8%, 15%, or whatever). Minimum and maximum levels might be established. A financial policy for the simulation may be "to maintain at least $50,000 in the cash account." These types of routine decisions are facilitated by establishing what the team wants to do *before* the fact; much time is saved thereby during the decision-making session.

A form is included in Chapter 7 for helping the team establish a few key policies in some of the more important areas.

COMPANY LOG

In order to provide continuity of decisions, each team may want to keep a log book containing some or all of the following items:

1. Organization chart
2. Objectives
3. Policies
4. Copy of each period's decision form
5. Written notes explaining the rationale of each quarter's decision
6. Comparative charts, graphs, or tables indicating the following quarterly information:
   a. Break-even analysis
   b. Cash position
   c. Dividends paid
   d. Profits and return on investment
   e. Marketing expenditure
   f. Price
   g. Plant size compared to quarterly production (for example, percent utilization
   h. Unit cost
   i. Ending inventory
   j. R & D expense
7. Copy of quarterly printout
8. Copy of justification of the incident decision
9. Any other information that would be of help in operating the firm

Different types of forms and charts are included in this manual to help the management team maintain the records needed for good decision making.

Self-Quiz

The objective of this quiz is to aid your understanding of the important aspects of the simulation. After reading over the preceding section twice, you should complete this quiz. A full understanding of the mechanics of the simulation is needed before making the first quarterly decision.

1. Each decision period simulated by the program is equal to a _____

   _____ (month, quarter, year).

2. What product is your firm selling? _____

3. What price has your firm been charging in the past quarters?_____

   _____

4. What factors affect sales for your firm?

   a. _____

   b. _____

   c. _____

   d. _____

   e. _____

5. The firm you are assuming management of:

   has been making _____ (modest, average, fairly high) profits.

   has a _____ (high, average, low) working capital position.

   has _____ (excessive, adequate, inadequate) production capacity.

6. Your firm will be evaluated on which of the following criteria?
   1. Cash position
   2. Inventory position
   3. Share of market
   4. Utilization of plant capacity
   5. Community citizenship
   6. Average stock price
   7. Net profits

a. 1 and 7
b. 3, 4, 5, 6, 7
c. 3, 6, 7
d. 1, 3, 4, 6, 7
e. all

7. Your plant currently has the capacity to produce _____ units per quarter.

8. Any units remaining unsold at the end of a quarter cost $_____ each in inventory cost. A mimimum inventory expense each quarter,

   regardless of the number of units on hand, is $_____.

9. The purpose of the production engineering budget is to
   a. produce a product with more consumer appeal.
   b. produce a higher quality product.
   c. produce a more innovative product.
   d. produce a lower cost product.

10. In the preceding quarter, the firm budgeted $_____ to the production engineering department.

11. Currently, the plant has the capacity to produce _____ units per quarter. In order to keep the capacity from decreasing each quarter,

    an amount equal to _____% of the plant investment must be reinvested each quarter. If greater capacity is needed, the firm would

    need to invest an additional $_____ per unit of additional capacity desired.

12. There is a lag of _____ quarter between the time you order additional plant capacity constructed and the availability of that extra capacity.

13. The optimum production level is the level of production that results in the lowest production cost per unit. The optimum production level for your particular plant is between
    a. 50 and 70% of capacity.
    b. 70 and 90% of capacity.
    c. 80 and 100% of capacity.
    d. None of the above

14. The research and development (R & D) budget for the firm was $_____

_____ last quarter. The objective of the R & D program is to _____

_____.

15. The success of an R & D program is related to its
   a. consistency.
   b. size of expenditure.
   c. durability.
   d. None of the above
   e. All of the above

16. Most fixed assets (Plant and Equipment in this simulation) have a limited useful life. The cost of such assets are charged as an expense

   in each accounting period. This accounting process is termed _____

   _____. The useful life of the fixed assets of your firm is _____

   years, and a charge of _____% per quarter is used to allocate

   this expense. This expense is a _____ (cash, noncash) item, so

   it _____ (is, is not) listed as a cash need on the cash analysis
   of the Quarterly Decision Worksheet.

17. The marketing program of the firm includes advertising, the sales force, and other promotional activities. The current budget for such expenses

   is $_____ per quarter.

18. At the present time, your firm is short of working capital (cash). Additional capital may be obtained through
   1. the sale of additional common stock.
   2. bank loans.
   3. the sale of bonds.
   4. the retention of earnings.
   a. 1
   b. 2
   c. 3
   d. 4
   e. 1, 2
   f. 1, 2, 3
   g. 1, 2, 4
   h. 2, 4
   i. 1, 4

19. The firm currently has _____ shares of common stock outstanding. Since _____ total shares are authorized by the firm's charter, the officers may sell an additional _____ shares of common stock and raise approximately $_____ of additional capital.

20. If the firm chooses to borrow from a bank, the loan may be taken for as long as _____ at an interest rate of _____% per _____ (quarter, year). The computer _____ (will, will not) automatically charge the interest to the company.

21. Each firm should plan the amount needed each quarter by using the _____. If a firm does not plan its cash well and has an overdraft in its cash account, the bank will cover the overdraft at an interest rate of _____% per quarter.

22. The Overhead and Fixed Expenses of the firm would include such items as officers' salaries, office and accounting expense, insurance, and property taxes. The current cost of such expenses is $_____ per quarter. This expense _____ (increases, decreases, remains constant) as production levels take certain specified increases.

23. If a firm does not pay dividends to stockholders, it will have more cash to invest in the business. However, such action may make the sale of additional stock difficult and/or cause the market price of the stock to _____ (decline, increase). On the other hand, a higher dividend would _____ (increase, decrease) the value of the stock, creating good stockholder and public relations. Your firm must decide on a dividend policy that is fair to the stockholder and optimizes company operations. Currently the firm is paying $_____ per share per quarter, costing a total of $_____ per quarter. At the current market price of $108 per share, this dividend equals a _____% per share return on the stockholder's investment.

ANSWERS TO THE SELF-QUIZ

1. quarter (13 weeks)

2. FM/AM auto radios

3. $40 per unit to the dealer

4. (a) General economic conditions; (b) Marketing expenditure;
   (c) R & D expense; (d) Price; (e) Competitors' decisions

5. modest; low; adequate

6. e

7. 24,250 units

8. $1.00; $1,000

9. d

10. $10,000

11. 24,250; 3%; $40

12. one quarter

13. b

14. $10,000; develop an improved product

15. e

16. depreciation; 8¼; 3%; noncash; is not

17. $90,000

18. g

19. 7,000; 12,000; $500,000

20. 3 years; 4% per quarter (16% per year); will

21. Quarterly Decision Worksheet; 7%

22. $100,000; increases

23. decline; increase; $1.00; $7,000;
    3.65% ($108 price ÷ $4.00 annual rate)

3

DECISION INCIDENTS

This chapter contains twelve incidents, one for each decision period. The incidents are numbered to correlate with the same decision period. For example, Incident # 1 is for Decision Period 1, Incident # 2 is for the second decision period, and so on.

Incident #1

The chairman of the board has asked the president of your firm to "get together with those boys over at Deitsville and see if we can't get the prices of our products up." The chairman is a close friend of the president of your firm, and the president was hand-picked for the presidency by the chairman. The president could be rightfully concerned about future relationships with the chairman if the matter is not handled delicately. The chairman's reference was to the company's strongest competitor in a city about 100 miles distant. Both firms have been making normal profits but have been going head-to-head as far as pricing is concerned.

The president knows the president of the Deitsville firm on a first-name basis, and he could talk to the other president with absolute confidentiality. Although price fixing is against federal laws, the president calculated the chances of being investigated and found them to be very slim. The price (and profits) of the firm could probably be increased by 10% without arousing suspicions. Which of the following actions should the president take?

1. Turn down the chairman unconditionally.

2. Talk to the president of the competing firm with no real intention of ever coming to an agreement on prices. This would then relieve the firm's president of his responsibility to the chairman of the board.

3. Enter into negotiations with the other president with extreme caution, with the intention of getting prices re-established at levels that will be more profitable to the firm.

Enter your decision 1, 2, or 3 on the decision form.

Incident #2

The management of your firm has received several requests from community organizations for funds. The requests have been listed at this time for a recommendation to be forwarded to the firm's board of directors. The following requests for funds have been made:

1. $10,000 for the local college. This is a small private college, the only one in the city where you are located, and it is fighting for its existence. The college is of no direct benefit to the company, except that once a year the firm sends four or five supervisors to a seminar the college sponsors. It is a four-year accredited school, offering mostly liberal arts courses, but it does have a business program. It is well thought of by citizens in the community but will probably continue to need additional support annually from the community to survive.

2. A request that the firm, along with its employees, participate in the annual United Appeal drive. The firm is being asked by the United Appeal to match dollar for dollar the contributions of the employees. Last year, the employees gave $6,000 to this drive.

3. A request of $5,000 from the city's Arts Committee to support various art activities. They include a children's summer art program, an art film festival, various concerts throughout the year from visiting musical groups, and the city's only museum.

4. A request from the Southside Neighborhood Association for a one-time grant of $8,000 to help construct a baseball field for Little League teams to be established in the area. The southside neighborhood is the area of the city containing the lower economic citizenry and some substandard housing.

For inputting your decision on the decision form, use the following table:

Amount Budgeted	Number To Record For Incident
$1,000 - $5,000	1
$5,100 - $11,000	2
$12,000 - $24,000	3
$29,000	4

Place the total amount budgeted in Other Expenses on the decision form *this* quarter.

© 1984 Houghton Mifflin Company

Incident #3

The production manager has submitted a request to the firm's officers to install pollution control equipment on the firm's smokestack and in its waste disposal system. Although the firm is not required to do so by law, the production manager feels the firm would be a better citizen in the community if it took these measures now instead of waiting until it was forced to do so. (It is thought such action could occur in one to three years.) Although most citizens of the community appreciate the firm's economic contribution to the community, many citizens are concerned about the plant polluting the water and the air in and around the city.

The production manager has estimated it will cost $100,000 for completion of the work and suggests that the contract be let immediately. The legal counsel has advised that although the firm is now within the federal guidelines for pollution, there is a 60% chance that further local or federal legislation will be forthcoming that will require more stringent pollution measures by the firm. The production manager is fairly sure the new equipment would meet any new regulations. Which of the following actions should the firm take?

1. Install the equipment. (Place $100,000 in Other Expenses on the decision form.)

2. Do not install the equipment.

3. Appoint a committee to study the situation during the coming year.

Enter your decision 1, 2, or 3 on the decision form.

Incident #4

The president of the firm has just discovered that in order to receive a substantial order each month, one of the salespersons is giving a fairly large kickback to the purchasing agent of Border Manufacturing. The firm's salespersons are paid a commission above their normal salary, and this particular salesman has been splitting his commission with the purchasing agent of the Border company. The sales manager has expressed great concern over losing the Border account if the kickback is discontinued. Although your sales manager does not approve of this arrangement, she does not offer an alternative to it. The Border account represents approximately 10% of your firm's business. The sales manager feels the probability of losing the entire Border account is about 90% if the kickback is discontinued. Which of the actions listed below should your firm take?

1. Discontinue the kickbacks and fire your salesman immediately.

2. Discontinue the kickbacks, and give your salesman a warning that if anything like this happens again, he will be discharged.

3. Take action 1 above, and notify the president of the Border company of the situation.

4. Take action 2 above, and notify the president of the Border company of the situation.

5. Do nothing at all about the situation.

Enter your decision 1, 2, 3, 4, or 5 on the decision form.

Incident #5

The personnel director of the company has just recommended to the firm's officers that a special training program be established for training and placing into employment the hard-core unemployed. Although the production plant of the firm is located in a medium-sized city, the city does have its share of the hard-core unemployed. At the present time, no governmental agencies have training programs for this group. However, it is thought that a training program will be established within the next year or two by the federal government. The firm's plant is located on the edge of town, about a mile from the low-income area from which the unemployed workers would be drawn. There is no public transportation, and the hard-core unemployed typically do not have transportation. Therefore, a privately owned school bus would be hired to pick up the workers in the morning and deliver them back to the area after the workday. It is felt that once the workers are trained and have had an opportunity to receive regular paychecks, the firm would no longer need to provide transportation. The personnel director estimates the cost of transporting the workers and the added training at $30,000. This would be in addition to the normal training costs of breaking in a new worker.

Such programs in other cities have experienced a retention rate of from 30 to 70%. However, the personnel director feels that with proper counseling, guidance, and encouragement, the retention rate for the group of 30 would be much higher than other companies have experienced. The firm pays competitive wages and has had no trouble in the past obtaining the workers it needs. The unemployment rate in the area is currently about 8%, with some veterans still trying to obtain jobs. The local minority action group has indicated it may take some action if the full program isn't implemented immediately. Your firm currently has about 150 production workers, but with an upturn in the economy anticipated, you do expect to need additional production workers. Which of the following actions should the company take?

1. Do not inaugurate the program.

2. After hiring all veterans and skilled workers available, begin hiring the hard-core unemployed as needed. No training program would be used.

3. Inaugurate the program on a smaller scale. (Place budget you want to allocate in Other Expenses on the decision form.)

4. Establish a committee to study the situation and make a recommendation within six months to a year.

5. Start the program immediately. (Place $30,000 in Other Expenses on the decision form.)

Enter your decision 1, 2, 3, 4, or 5 on the decision form.

Incident #6

The vice president for manufacturing has just informed the management team of the firm that there is a substantial inventory of last year's model. Although the previous year's model does not differ externally from the current year's model, there were substantial improvements made internally. One of the members suggests that the nameplates for the current model be placed on last year's model, and that they be sold as current models. Management realizes that they will probably have to sell the inventory at less than cost in order to move it out, because the current model is of substantially higher quality than the previous model. The firm would stand to lose about $50,000 on the inventory. (For purposes of this incident, assume your firm has substantial inventory, regardless of your actual inventory position.)

Which of the following actions should the firm take?

1. Change the nameplate and sell the inventory as the current year's product.

2. Sell the inventory as last year's model at the best possible price. (Place $50,000 in Other Expenses on the decision form.)

3. Remove the nameplate from last year's model; do *not* put on this year's nameplate but hope that purchasers will *assume* it is current because of the similarity.

Enter your decision 1, 2, or 3 on the decision form.

Incident #7

The president of the firm has just entered into a meeting with the vice president of sales and the advertising manager.

"Joe, that new advertising campaign that the Brown agency has created is really doing a spectacular job for our product," the president exclaims. "But I was reading some of the specifications the advertising claimed, and I just don't believe our product meets those specifications."

"Well, Mr. Jay," the advertising manager explains, "those specifications do seem a bit high to me too, but consider it just harmless trade puffery. You know everyone else is doing that type of thing now."

"Yes," the sales manager says, "it certainly has been a successful ad and our sales are up over 20% from last year. You can't fault that."

The president continues, "We do not meet the specifications, and I don't feel that we should use them in our ads."

"Well, Mr. Jay," the advertising manager says, "to tell you the truth, it's those promises that the ad makes about our specifications that are really selling this product."

"But," the president says, "how about the statement about our warranty? The ad states we have the best warranty in the industry, and that just simply is not true. Why, our warranty is the same as everyone else's in the industry."

"Well, 'best' means different things to different people," the sales vice president explains. "And I don't think we could be taken to court on that."

"Well," the president says, "this whole situation should be discussed by the management team, and recommendations one way or the other should be made."

Which of the following actions should the firm take?

1. Instruct the advertising agency to keep the claims about the specifications of the product exactly as they really are.

2. Cancel the contract with the advertising agency and place the contract with another firm.

3. Try advertising without the claims in a test market.

4. Allow the ad campaign to continue as it is currently running.

5. Tell the advertising agency to tone down the claims slightly in order to appease the president.

6. After considerable discussion, vote to turn the problem back to the advertising manager for him to take whatever action he sees fit.

Enter your decision 1, 2, 3, 4, 5, or 6 on the decision form.

Incident #8

For years your firm has purchased plastic cases for your product from a small plastics manufacturer. The manufacturer in fact built a small factory adjacent to your firm's factory, and 100% of the production from the plastics factory has been for your firm's plastic cases. Relationships with this company have been excellent, deliveries are made on time, and liberal credit terms have always been available. Both parties have been extremely satisfied with the arrangement. Now, however, a foreign firm approaches your firm with a bid for your business that is 15% lower than that of your present supplier. Although the shipping time would be increased considerably and your firm would need to buy much larger lots at one time, the total savings considering these factors would still amount to $40,000 to $50,000 per year. The foreign firm has a large plant in Japan, the capacity to serve your firm, and very minor labor problems. It is felt the firm could deliver the goods satisfactorily. Upon presenting the supplier with the situation and the price differential, that firm's president insists that no price concession can be made. "In fact," he states, "we have absorbed, several times, small raw-material price increases in order not to raise the price to you."

He also mentions that if your firm ceases buying from his, he will have to close his factory, and that if that occurs he will be willing to sell his factory to your firm. He feels $200,000 is a fair price for the plant and equipment. Two members of your management team feel that you should not get into the plastic molding business, as you do not have the know-how. Another member feels the purchase of the plant next door would be a wise move and that you could produce the casings for the same price the foreign firm is quoting. Another officer makes a strong plea for continuing the arrangement with the firm you have always done business with, saying that it's definitely worth a little more to be assured of a high-quality product and timely delivery. Which of the following actions should your firm take?

1. Give the casing contract to the foreign firm.

2. Continue the present arrangement with the current supplier.

3. Cancel the contract with the present supplier and offer to purchase his plant for $100,000.

4. Cancel the contract with the present supplier and offer to purchase his plant for $200,000.

Enter your decision 1, 2, 3, or 4 on the decision form.

Incident #9

Senator DeBigg has just left the corporate offices of your firm. He is running for re-election in the fall and has asked your firm for a donation of $50,000 to help his campaign. Senator DeBigg is chairman of the State Senate Committee, which can affect legislation resulting in contracts potentially beneficial to your firm in the next few years. The firm's legal counsel has advised that corporations may not make political contributions and that to do so would be illegal. Various members of the corporate management team have suggested that the corporation give the contribution through a foundation or an industry-operated educational fund. Both of these methods would result in the firm facing prosecution if discovered. (Estimates have been made that if the new legislation were passed, the firm could expect an increase in sales of from 8 to 15%.) The passage of the legislation is almost assured if Senator DeBigg is re-elected. Indicate which of the following actions your firm should take.

1. Turn down Mr. DeBigg altogether.

2. Ask the corporate officers to make donations to his campaign. (This is legal.)

3. Increase each corporate officer's salary by $6,000, so that each may contribute a net of $4,000 to Senator DeBigg's campaign. This would total $24,000 for the campaign (also legal). (Place $36,000 in Other Expenses.)

4. Make the full contribution of $50,000 through the foundation or industry educational fund after the conclusion has been reached that the probability of being caught is only about 5%. (Place $50,000 in Other Expenses.)

Enter your decision 1, 2, 3, or 4 on the decision form.

Incident #10

During a recent meeting of the management of your firm, the sales manager requested that she be allowed to hire one of the top salesmen from a competing firm. She feels that the salesman can be lured away with the promise of a $35,000 salary, which is somewhat more than he is receiving from the other firm. The sales manager claims the salesman could retain at least half of his customers if he were to come to work for your firm.

Much discussion ensued during the meeting as to the morality of hiring the salesman away from another firm for the specific purpose of obtaining that firm's customers. It was also mentioned that other firms might do the same to your firm. In the middle of the discussion, the production manager stated that if this were going to be an approved company policy, he would also like to hire the key production engineer away from another competitor. This particular production engineer installed many innovative production techniques and was able to effect at least a 5% production cost savings for the competing firm. As a result, the competing firm was able to be the most competitive in the firm's industry. He felt the production engineer could be hired at an annual rate of $40,000 plus participation in the officers' stock option plan. Which of the following actions should the firm take?

1. Hire both men.

2. Hire the salesman only.

3. Hire the engineer only.

4. Hire neither.

Enter your choice 1, 2, 3, or 4 on the decision form.

Incident #11

The sales manager of the firm has worked diligently in finally obtaining a large chain store account. The chain store has agreed to place a large order (amounting to 10% of your firm's total business) if the firm will manufacture a special model for the chain store exclusively. This model would contain fewer transistors than the company's usual product. By doing this, the cost savings could be passed on to the chain store in the form of a lower price, and the chain store in turn could sell the product at a higher margin. However, the chain insists that the product must have the exact appearance, nameplate, and markings as the company's regular product. Two of the corporate officers have spoken in favor of the arrangement, stating that the general public wouldn't know the difference and the performance of the product would probably not be altered that greatly. Other officers feel it is definitely wrong to accept the proposal. Still others have simply shrugged their shoulders and said, "If we don't do it, someone else will." What action should the company take?

1. Reject the proposal from the chain store.

2. Accept the proposal.

3. Offer the chain store the lesser product with the regular nameplate and model number but a different case design.

Enter your decision 1, 2, or 3 on the decision form.

Incident #12

A large customer in the Greater New York area has demanded that it become the exclusive distributor of your product in its area. Currently, that firm purchases about 5% of your total sales. If you agree to this demand, it will mean losing the other customer in the area, which has been purchasing from your firm since its establishment. The smaller firm represents about 1% of your total sales. The larger firm insists it must have exclusive rights and will cease doing business with your company if it does not obtain these rights. If the larger firm does cancel, you could expect that the smaller firm would increase its sales somewhat. The profit margin of both accounts are equal. What should your firm do?

1. Cancel your present sales agreement with the smaller firm and grant exclusive sales rights to the larger firm in the New York area.

2. Cancel your present sales agreement with the smaller firm and grant exclusive sales rights to the larger firm in the New York area if the larger firm agrees to purchase a 6% share, thereby replacing the loss of the smaller firm.

3. Attempt to talk the large firm out of its demand; if that fails, let them go rather than jeopardize the position of the smaller buyer.

Enter your decision 1, 2, or 3 on the decision form.

4

LOG OF COMPANY DECISIONS

As your firm makes decisions through the simulation, you may need to alter your strategy to meet competitive and/or economic changes. It is recommended that you record your actions each quarter on this form *and* the rationale for your decisions. You will then have a record to help you fine tune your future decisions. Keep a copy of the actual numbers you input on Form R-5 in Chapter 7.

Period 1

Period 2

_____

_____

_____

_____

_____

_____

_____

_____

_____

_____

_____

_____

_____

_____

_____

_____

_____

_____

_____

_____

Period 3

_____

_____

_____

_____

_____

_____

_____

_____

_____

_____

_____

_____

_____

_____

_____

_____

_____

_____

_____

_____

Period 4

Period 5

_____

_____

_____

_____

_____

_____

_____

_____

_____

_____

_____

_____

_____

_____

_____

_____

_____

_____

_____

Period 6

_____

_____

_____

_____

_____

_____

_____

_____

_____

_____

_____

_____

_____

_____

_____

_____

_____

_____

_____

_____

_____

Period 7

Period 8

Period 9

_____

_____

_____

_____

_____

_____

_____

_____

_____

_____

_____

_____

_____

_____

_____

_____

_____

_____

_____

_____

_____

_____

Period 10

Period 11

Period 12

5

INTERNAL MANAGEMENT AUDIT

The purpose of this audit is to have you review your team's results at any given point during the simulation. This will help your team to optimize future decisions. See form A-1, page 61.

Your instructor may want this audit accomplished sometime during the half-way point of play or perhaps after the simulation ends. Even if it is not a required activity, your team should evaluate its actions at least once during the simulation in order to ascertain if what you have been doing is the most appropriate action. This is a good example of the *control* function of the manager. You have *planned* your objectives for the simulation, *organized* the resources of your management team and of the simulation company, made *decisions* in *directing* the activities of the simulation firm, and to some extent, *controlled* the firm through financial analysis. At this point, it would be wise to make a thorough quantitative and qualitative evaluation of (1) your management team (even though it may be only yourself!) and (2) your simulation company.

To emphasize the point: the purpose of this audit is to have you review your company's results through a particular quarter of play, compare them with your thinking about the game when you started, and make any changes you deem desirable in order to improve both your team's performance and your own individual learning. If the audit comes during the simulation's midpoint of play, you still have time to take corrective action. If the audit is done at the end of simulation play, your conclusions will be more in the form of a report card as to your success. Especially of interest in this latter case is the response to the audit question, "If you had the opportunity to start all over again, what would you do differently?" The *audit guide* shown below is just that — a guide. There are other questions and approaches to this activity. Just remember that the audit is *not* a typical accounting-type audit but rather a *management* audit and should be approached as such.

Some other approaches and topics that could be involved in looking at your team and company operation include the following:

1. Select one major area that you feel presents a major problem for your team. It might be a lack of sales or, conversely, stocking-out of the product frequently. It could be a matter of not understanding the interrelationships among prices, marketing, R & D, and sales. These are just a few examples; there are certainly others. Analyze the problem, present alternative solutions, and select the solution that you will (or would) implement in order to improve your company's performance from this point forward.

2. If your team has more than one person, you could select a major area in which your team is having a problem and work out a strategy for solving that problem. One example might be needing to communicate effectively with one another to maximize understanding of one another's views. An-

other might be how to make group decisions better (with fewer arguments). Still another might be to admit that one or more group members need help in understanding the financial portions of the printout.

3. Review the Log of Company Decisions for all quarters up to the present. Do these records clearly indicate the rationale for the decisions you have made in past quarters? Have you made assumptions that are no longer valid? Do your records support your actions?

4. Review your initial mission statement, objectives, and policies. Even if you did not write these down, you can ask, "What was our original strategy? Are we still on course?" If your planning was recorded, you can ask such questions as the following:

   a. Are we achieving our objectives? If not, why not? What changes can we make to improve the possibilities of achieving our goals?

   b. Can we measure the progress we are making (or have made) toward achieving our objectives? If not, perhaps we can restate our objectives in more *specific* terms so that we can determine whether we achieved our objectives at some future measuring point.

   c. Are our policies helping us to achieve our objectives? Are we following policies even though they are not formally stated? Should we clarify what we are doing by thinking through these unwritten policies and formally writing them out as policy? Are we not utilizing some of our original policies? Should they be updated? changed?

   d. Are we following the strategies we initially established (whether written or verbal)? Do new strategies appear to be needed?

5. If you are doing this audit during the simulation play and not at the end, you might consider the following idea. Revise the interpersonal roles you each play within your team. For example, if one person is the low-key, nonverbal type, he or she might be encouraged to play a more active role. Of course, the talkers of the team will need to take a more passive role and listen more attentively. The object is to try and participate in a manner that is not your normal pattern and experience your feelings about being in this different role.

The key element of the management audit is to *learn* something about yourself, your company, or others that will help you understand the real world in a more effective manner.

© 1984 Houghton Mifflin Company

Form A-1: Management Audit

Company _____
Prepared after Quarter No. _____

1. Does the firm have well-defined and adequately stated objectives?

2. Does the firm have a prudent dividend policy? For example, would you be satisfied with the dividends that have been paid if you were a stockholder?

3. Did the team make decisions on a rational basis or did it often "stab in the dark" in making decisions?

4. Has the firm been able to produce at optimum production levels (70 to 90%) consistently?

5. Have research and development expenditures been adequate? consistent?

6. Have production engineering expenditures been adequate? consistent?

7. Has the firm been able to adjust marketing and production decisions in order to have an optimum inventory? *Optimum* could be defined as enough inventory to cover sales in case the plant were to have an unscheduled stoppage, perhaps two to four weeks of sales, and yet not be so large as to cost substantial inventory carrying charges.

8. How many times has the firm ended a quarter with zero units in inventory, thus losing sales?

9. Did the firm plan its cash needs well in order to prevent either an excess amount of cash or not enough cash to meet current demand? Explain.

10. How many times has the firm ended with a zero cash balance?

11. Were the pricing decisions consistent? prudent?

12. At this point, is the firm a healthy, going concern? Explain.

13. If you had the opportunity to start all over again, what would you do differently?

6

BREAK-EVEN ANALYSIS

Break-even analysis is a method of determining the minimum sales volume required to cover all costs at a given price level. A more detailed explanation and worksheets are included in this chapter.

A commonly used control tool used by managers is the break-even analysis. This analysis generates information that illustrates various levels of profit or loss associated with various levels of production and sales. The basic question to be addressed is: "What is the lowest level of production and sales that the firm can be at and still break even?" In other words, at what sales level does total revenue equal total costs? Other questions arise naturally from this first question, such as: "If we can make x dollars profit at our current level of sales, what profits might we assume at some other level of sales (either higher or lower)?"

Two Methods of Analysis

There are two methods of approaching the break-even problem. One is the algebraic method, and the other is the graphic method. Both are described below in enough detail to allow the participant to use this tool to increase the quality of decisions in the simulation.

ALGEBRAIC BREAK-EVEN FORMULA

$$\frac{\text{Total fixed costs}}{\text{Current price} - \text{Variable cost of each unit sold}} = \text{Break-even level}$$

In this formula, the variable cost would equal the Manufacturing Cost as listed on the bottom of the firm's printout. (A word about "Total fixed cost" in the formula above: In this simulation, many of the costs we are going to call fixed costs are somewhat variable in that management can vary the amount for the budget in that area, for example, marketing expense. However, since most of these selling and administrative expenses are necessary to support a given level of sales, we are going to treat them as fixed expenses. For the purposes here, consider the Fixed Cost to be all costs from the current Income and Expense Statement on the printout *except* Cost of Goods Sold.)

Using the data from the Quarter 0 printout, the following would be obtained:

$$\frac{\text{Total fixed costs (all expenses except Cost of Goods Sold)}}{\text{Price (\$40)} - \text{Variable cost (\$23.52)}}$$

$$= \frac{254,000}{40.00 - 23.52} = 15,352$$

The break-even point would be 15,352 units. This indicates that if expenses and the sales price remain constant, the firm would incur a loss if radio sales are fewer than 15,352 units. To state it another way, it takes that many units to cover the current Fixed Cost of the firm.

GRAPHIC BREAK-EVEN METHOD

This method gives the manager a more complete picture of the cumulative relationships among *all* the factors that go into product cost and profits. The potential profit or loss can quickly be determined at various levels of sales with this method. The chart below shows not only the same information as the method above but also has the greater utility of giving additional information at other possible sales levels.

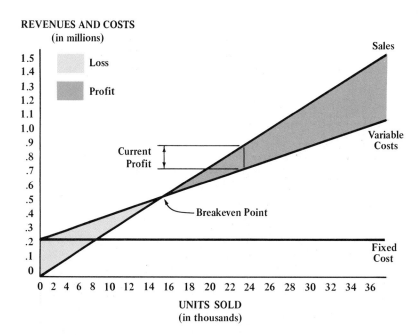

Form B-7: Break-even Analysis

COMPANY NO. _____ QUARTER NO. _____

PREPARED BY _____

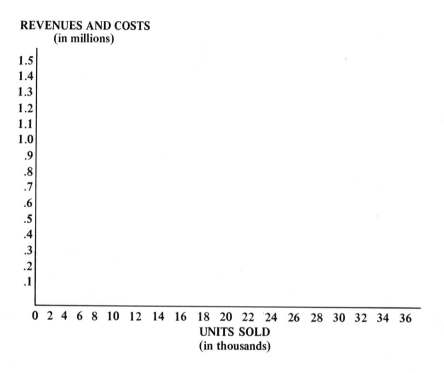

REVENUES AND COSTS
(in millions)

Break-even Formula

$$\frac{\text{Total fixed costs}^1}{\text{Current price} - \text{Variable cost}^2} = \underline{\hspace{3cm}} = \underline{\hspace{2cm}} \text{ units}$$

[1] All expenses except Cost of Goods Sold
[2] Same as Manufacturing Cost

Form B-7: Break-even Analysis

COMPANY NO. _____ QUARTER NO. _____

PREPARED BY _____

REVENUES AND COSTS
(in millions)

UNITS SOLD
(in thousands)

Break-even Formula

$$\frac{\text{Total fixed costs}^1}{\text{Current price} - \text{Variable cost}^2} = \underline{\hspace{3cm}} = \underline{\hspace{2cm}} \text{ units}$$

[1] All expenses except Cost of Goods Sold
[2] Same as Manufacturing Cost

Form B-7:   Break-even Analysis

COMPANY NO. _____ QUARTER NO. _____

PREPARED BY _____

REVENUES AND COSTS
    (in millions)

```
1.5 |
1.4 |
1.3 |
1.2 |
1.1 |
1.0 |
 .9 |
 .8 |
 .7 |
 .6 |
 .5 |
 .4 |
 .3 |
 .2 |
 .1 |
    |_____
     0  2  4  6  8  10  12  14  16  18  20  22  24  26  28  30  32  34  36
```
                          UNITS SOLD
                          (in thousands)

Break-even Formula

$$\frac{\text{Total fixed costs}^1}{\text{Current price} - \text{Variable cost}^2} = \underline{\hspace{2cm}} = \underline{\hspace{1.5cm}} \text{ units}$$

[1]All expenses except Cost of Goods Sold
[2]Same as Manufacturing Cost

Form B-7:   Break-even Analysis

COMPANY NO. _____ QUARTER NO. _____

PREPARED BY _____

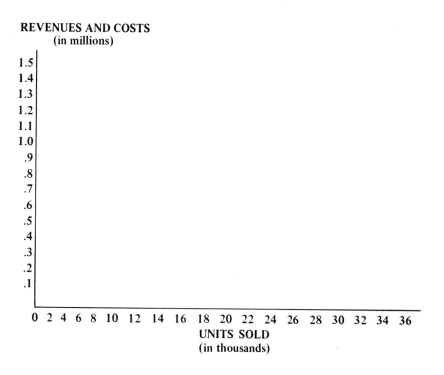

REVENUES AND COSTS
(in millions)

1.5
1.4
1.3
1.2
1.1
1.0
.9
.8
.7
.6
.5
.4
.3
.2
.1

0 2 4 6 8 10 12 14 16 18 20 22 24 26 28 30 32 34 36

UNITS SOLD
(in thousands)

Break-even Formula

$$\frac{\text{Total fixed costs}^1}{\text{Current price} - \text{Variable cost}^2} = \underline{\hspace{2cm}} = \underline{\hspace{1.5cm}} \text{ units}$$

[1]All expenses except Cost of Goods Sold
[2]Same as Manufacturing Cost

Form B-7: Break-even Analysis

COMPANY NO. _____ QUARTER NO. _____

PREPARED BY _____

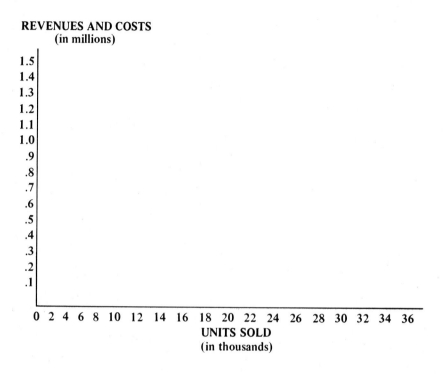

REVENUES AND COSTS
(in millions)

Break-even Formula

$$\frac{\text{Total fixed costs}^1}{\text{Current price} - \text{Variable cost}^2} = \underline{\hspace{3cm}} = \underline{\hspace{2cm}} \text{ units}$$

[1]All expenses except Cost of Goods Sold
[2]Same as Manufacturing Cost

7

MANAGEMENT INFORMATION

This chapter contains several different types of forms and charts to help the team in maintaining the management information needed for making better-informed decisions.

Form OB-1: Corporate Mission, Objectives, and Strategy

Corporate Mission (or purpose): _____

_____

Objective # 1: _____

    Strategy (or Action Plan) to accomplish this objective: _____

    _____

    _____

    Policy (or policies) to aid in implementing this objective: _____

    _____

    _____

Objective # 2: _____

    Strategy (or Action Plan) to accomplish this objective: _____

    _____

    _____

    Policy (or policies) to aid in implementing this objective: _____

    _____

    _____

Objective # 3: _____

    Strategy (or Action Plan) to accomplish this objective: _____

    _____

    _____

    Policy (or policies) to aid in implementing this objective: _____

    _____

    _____

Note: This form is illustrative of the hierarchy of corporate planning. It should be amended as necessary for planning within your own firm.

Form MC-2:   Manufacturing Cost Data

Period Number	Production Capacity (Column 1)	Actual Production (Column 2)	Production Utilization (Col. 1 ÷ Col. 2)	Production Engineering Budget	Per- Unit Cost
0	25,000	25,000	100%	$ 10,000	$23.52
1					
2					
3					
4					
5					
6					
7					
8					
9					
10					
11					
12					

Form S-3:   Marketing Data Analysis

Period Number	Marketing Budget	R & D Budget	Current Price	Sales (in units)	% Increase or Decrease over Previous Period
0	$90,000	$10,000	$40.00	23,062	
1					
2					
3					
4					
5					
6					
7					
8					
9					
10					
11					
12					

Form SP-4: Dividend and Stock Price Chart

Column	1	2	3	4	5
Period Number	Shares Outstanding	Total Dividends Paid	Dividends Paid per Share (Col. 2 ÷ Col. 1)	Current Stock Price	Return on Investment: Annualized (4 x Col. 3 ÷ Col. 4)
0	7,000	$7,000	$ 1.00	108	3.6%
1					
2					
3					
4					
5					
6					
7					
8					
9					
10					
11					
12					

Form R-5: Record of Quarterly Decisions

Period Number	Price	Mkt.	Prod: Units	Prod. Engr.	R & D	Plant Addtn.	Divi-dends	Other Exp.	Bank Loan	Stock Sold	Inci-dent
0	40	90	25000	10	10	30	7	0	0	0	0
1											
2											
3											
4											
5											
6											
7											
8											
9											
10											
11											
12											

8

WORKSHEETS AND DECISION FORMS

This chapter contains multiple copies of three different worksheets as well as the quarterly decision form.

Form F-6:   Selected Financial Ratios

COMPANY NO. _____ QUARTER NO. _____

PREPARED BY _____

1. Debt-to-Equity Ratio

$$\frac{\text{Loans Payable}}{\text{Common Stock + Retained Earnings}} \qquad \text{_____} = \text{_____}$$

2. Inventory Turnover

$$\frac{\text{Cost of Goods Sold}}{\text{Inventory (\$)}} \qquad \text{_____} = \text{_____}$$

3. Gross Margin

$$\frac{\text{Sales} - \text{Cost of Goods Sold}}{\text{Sales}} \qquad \text{_____} = \text{_____}$$

4. Sales Margin (Return on Sales)

$$\frac{\text{Net Profit after Taxes}}{\text{Sales}} \qquad \text{_____} = \text{_____}$$

5. Return on Assets

$$\frac{\text{Net Profit after Taxes}}{\text{Total Assets}} \qquad \text{_____} = \text{_____}$$

6. Return on Net Worth

$$\frac{\text{Net Profit after Taxes}}{\text{Common Stock + Retained Earnings}} \qquad \text{_____} = \text{_____}$$

Form F-6:   Selected Financial Ratios

COMPANY NO. _____ QUARTER NO. _____

PREPARED BY _____

1. Debt-to-Equity Ratio

$$\frac{\text{Loans Payable}}{\text{Common Stock + Retained Earnings}} \qquad \underline{\hspace{2cm}} = \underline{\hspace{2cm}}$$

2. Inventory Turnover

$$\frac{\text{Cost of Goods Sold}}{\text{Inventory (\$)}} \qquad \underline{\hspace{2cm}} = \underline{\hspace{2cm}}$$

3. Gross Margin

$$\frac{\text{Sales} - \text{Cost of Goods Sold}}{\text{Sales}} \qquad \underline{\hspace{2cm}} = \underline{\hspace{2cm}}$$

4. Sales Margin (Return on Sales)

$$\frac{\text{Net Profit after Taxes}}{\text{Sales}} \qquad \underline{\hspace{2cm}} = \underline{\hspace{2cm}}$$

5. Return on Assets

$$\frac{\text{Net Profit after Taxes}}{\text{Total Assets}} \qquad \underline{\hspace{2cm}} = \underline{\hspace{2cm}}$$

6. Return on Net Worth

$$\frac{\text{Net Profit after Taxes}}{\text{Common Stock + Retained Earnings}} \qquad \underline{\hspace{2cm}} = \underline{\hspace{2cm}}$$

Form F-6: Selected Financial Ratios

COMPANY NO. _____ QUARTER NO. _____

PREPARED BY _____

1. Debt-to-Equity Ratio

$$\frac{\text{Loans Payable}}{\text{Common Stock + Retained Earnings}} \qquad \underline{\hspace{2cm}} = \underline{\hspace{2cm}}$$

2. Inventory Turnover

$$\frac{\text{Cost of Goods Sold}}{\text{Inventory (\$)}} \qquad \underline{\hspace{2cm}} = \underline{\hspace{2cm}}$$

3. Gross Margin

$$\frac{\text{Sales} - \text{Cost of Goods Sold}}{\text{Sales}} \qquad \underline{\hspace{2cm}} = \underline{\hspace{2cm}}$$

4. Sales Margin (Return on Sales)

$$\frac{\text{Net Profit after Taxes}}{\text{Sales}} \qquad \underline{\hspace{2cm}} = \underline{\hspace{2cm}}$$

5. Return on Assets

$$\frac{\text{Net Profit after Taxes}}{\text{Total Assets}} \qquad \underline{\hspace{2cm}} = \underline{\hspace{2cm}}$$

6. Return on Net Worth

$$\frac{\text{Net Profit after Taxes}}{\text{Common Stock + Retained Earnings}} \qquad \underline{\hspace{2cm}} = \underline{\hspace{2cm}}$$

Form F-6:   Selected Financial Ratios

COMPANY NO. _____ QUARTER NO. _____

PREPARED BY _____

1. Debt-to-Equity Ratio

$$\frac{\text{Loans Payable}}{\text{Common Stock} + \text{Retained Earnings}}$$ _____ = _____

2. Inventory Turnover

$$\frac{\text{Cost of Goods Sold}}{\text{Inventory (\$)}}$$ _____ = _____

3. Gross Margin

$$\frac{\text{Sales} - \text{Cost of Goods Sold}}{\text{Sales}}$$ _____ = _____

4. Sales Margin (Return on Sales)

$$\frac{\text{Net Profit after Taxes}}{\text{Sales}}$$ _____ = _____

5. Return on Assets

$$\frac{\text{Net Profit after Taxes}}{\text{Total Assets}}$$ _____ = _____

6. Return on Net Worth

$$\frac{\text{Net Profit after Taxes}}{\text{Common Stock} + \text{Retained Earnings}}$$ _____ = _____

Form F-6: Selected Financial Ratios

COMPANY NO. _____ QUARTER NO. _____

PREPARED BY _____

1. Debt-to-Equity Ratio

$$\frac{\text{Loans Payable}}{\text{Common Stock + Retained Earnings}} \qquad \rule{3cm}{0.4pt} = \rule{3cm}{0.4pt}$$

2. Inventory Turnover

$$\frac{\text{Cost of Goods Sold}}{\text{Inventory (\$)}} \qquad \rule{3cm}{0.4pt} = \rule{3cm}{0.4pt}$$

3. Gross Margin

$$\frac{\text{Sales} - \text{Cost of Goods Sold}}{\text{Sales}} \qquad \rule{3cm}{0.4pt} = \rule{3cm}{0.4pt}$$

4. Sales Margin (Return on Sales)

$$\frac{\text{Net Profit after Taxes}}{\text{Sales}} \qquad \rule{3cm}{0.4pt} = \rule{3cm}{0.4pt}$$

5. Return on Assets

$$\frac{\text{Net Profit after Taxes}}{\text{Total Assets}} \qquad \rule{3cm}{0.4pt} = \rule{3cm}{0.4pt}$$

6. Return on Net Worth

$$\frac{\text{Net Profit after Taxes}}{\text{Common Stock + Retained Earnings}} \qquad \rule{3cm}{0.4pt} = \rule{3cm}{0.4pt}$$

Form F-6:   Selected Financial Ratios

COMPANY NO. _____ QUARTER NO. _____

PREPARED BY _____

1. Debt-to-Equity Ratio

$$\frac{\text{Loans Payable}}{\text{Common Stock + Retained Earnings}} \qquad \underline{\hspace{2cm}} = \underline{\hspace{2cm}}$$

2. Inventory Turnover

$$\frac{\text{Cost of Goods Sold}}{\text{Inventory (\$)}} \qquad \underline{\hspace{2cm}} = \underline{\hspace{2cm}}$$

3. Gross Margin

$$\frac{\text{Sales} - \text{Cost of Goods Sold}}{\text{Sales}} \qquad \underline{\hspace{2cm}} = \underline{\hspace{2cm}}$$

4. Sales Margin (Return on Sales)

$$\frac{\text{Net Profit after Taxes}}{\text{Sales}} \qquad \underline{\hspace{2cm}} = \underline{\hspace{2cm}}$$

5. Return on Assets

$$\frac{\text{Net Profit after Taxes}}{\text{Total Assets}} \qquad \underline{\hspace{2cm}} = \underline{\hspace{2cm}}$$

6. Return on Net Worth

$$\frac{\text{Net Profit after Taxes}}{\text{Common Stock + Retained Earnings}} \qquad \underline{\hspace{2cm}} = \underline{\hspace{2cm}}$$

Form F-6: Selected Financial Ratios

COMPANY NO. _____ QUARTER NO. _____

PREPARED BY _____

1. Debt-to-Equity Ratio

$$\frac{\text{Loans Payable}}{\text{Common Stock + Retained Earnings}}$$ _____ = _____

2. Inventory Turnover

$$\frac{\text{Cost of Goods Sold}}{\text{Inventory (\$)}}$$ _____ = _____

3. Gross Margin

$$\frac{\text{Sales – Cost of Goods Sold}}{\text{Sales}}$$ _____ = _____

4. Sales Margin (Return on Sales)

$$\frac{\text{Net Profit after Taxes}}{\text{Sales}}$$ _____ = _____

5. Return on Assets

$$\frac{\text{Net Profit after Taxes}}{\text{Total Assets}}$$ _____ = _____

6. Return on Net Worth

$$\frac{\text{Net Profit after Taxes}}{\text{Common Stock + Retained Earnings}}$$ _____ = _____

Form F-6:   Selected Financial Ratios

COMPANY NO. _____ QUARTER NO. _____

PREPARED BY _____

1. Debt-to-Equity Ratio

$$\frac{\text{Loans Payable}}{\text{Common Stock + Retained Earnings}} \qquad \underline{\hspace{3cm}} = \underline{\hspace{3cm}}$$

2. Inventory Turnover

$$\frac{\text{Cost of Goods Sold}}{\text{Inventory (\$)}} \qquad \underline{\hspace{3cm}} = \underline{\hspace{3cm}}$$

3. Gross Margin

$$\frac{\text{Sales} - \text{Cost of Goods Sold}}{\text{Sales}} \qquad \underline{\hspace{3cm}} = \underline{\hspace{3cm}}$$

4. Sales Margin (Return on Sales)

$$\frac{\text{Net Profit after Taxes}}{\text{Sales}} \qquad \underline{\hspace{3cm}} = \underline{\hspace{3cm}}$$

5. Return on Assets

$$\frac{\text{Net Profit after Taxes}}{\text{Total Assets}} \qquad \underline{\hspace{3cm}} = \underline{\hspace{3cm}}$$

6. Return on Net Worth

$$\frac{\text{Net Profit after Taxes}}{\text{Common Stock + Retained Earnings}} \qquad \underline{\hspace{3cm}} = \underline{\hspace{3cm}}$$

Form F-6: Selected Financial Ratios

COMPANY NO. _____ QUARTER NO. _____

PREPARED BY _____

1. Debt-to-Equity Ratio

$$\frac{\text{Loans Payable}}{\text{Common Stock + Retained Earnings}} \qquad \underline{\hspace{2cm}} = \underline{\hspace{2cm}}$$

2. Inventory Turnover

$$\frac{\text{Cost of Goods Sold}}{\text{Inventory (\$)}} \qquad \underline{\hspace{2cm}} = \underline{\hspace{2cm}}$$

3. Gross Margin

$$\frac{\text{Sales} - \text{Cost of Goods Sold}}{\text{Sales}} \qquad \underline{\hspace{2cm}} = \underline{\hspace{2cm}}$$

4. Sales Margin (Return on Sales)

$$\frac{\text{Net Profit after Taxes}}{\text{Sales}} \qquad \underline{\hspace{2cm}} = \underline{\hspace{2cm}}$$

5. Return on Assets

$$\frac{\text{Net Profit after Taxes}}{\text{Total Assets}} \qquad \underline{\hspace{2cm}} = \underline{\hspace{2cm}}$$

6. Return on Net Worth

$$\frac{\text{Net Profit after Taxes}}{\text{Common Stock + Retained Earnings}} \qquad \underline{\hspace{2cm}} = \underline{\hspace{2cm}}$$

Form P-7: Product Cost and Profit Analysis

COMPANY NO. _____ QUARTER NO. _____

PREPARED BY _____

1. Current Selling Price . . . .   _____._____

2. Per-Unit Production Cost
    e.g., Variable Cost (from printout) . . . .   _____._____

3. Contribution Margin
    (Item 1 − 2) . . . .   _____._____

4. Production   Units
    Engineering   Sold:
    $_____ ÷ _____ = _____._____

5. Inventory   Units
    Expense: Sold:
    $_____ ÷ _____ = _____._____

6. Marketing   Units
    Expense: Sold:
    $_____ ÷ _____ = _____._____

7. R & D   Units
    Expense: Sold:
    $_____ ÷ _____ = _____._____

8. Interest   Units
    Expense: Sold:
    $_____ ÷ _____ = _____._____

9. Depreciation   Units
    Expense: Sold:
    $_____ ÷ _____ = _____._____

10. Total Cost: Per Unit
    (Items 2 and 4 through 9)   _____._____

11. Gross Profit per Unit (Price less Total Cost)   _____._____

12. Overhead: Units Sold:
    $_____ ÷ _____ =   _____._____

13. Profit per Unit (Before Taxes) . . . .   _____._____
    (Item 11 less item 12)

Form P-7:   Product Cost and Profit Analysis

COMPANY NO. _____ QUARTER NO. _____

PREPARED BY _____ .

1. Current Selling Price . . . .   _____._____

2. Per-Unit Production Cost
    e.g., Variable Cost (from printout) . . . .   _____._____

3. Contribution Margin
    (Item 1 − 2) . . . .   _____._____

4. Production   Units
    Engineering   Sold:
    $_____   ÷   _____   =   _____._____

5. Inventory   Units
    Expense: Sold:
    $_____   ÷   _____   =   _____._____

6. Marketing   Units
    Expense: Sold:
    $_____   ÷   _____   =   _____._____

7. R & D   Units
    Expense: Sold:
    $_____   ÷   _____   =   _____._____

8. Interest   Units
    Expense: Sold:
    $_____   ÷   _____   =   _____._____

9. Depreciation   Units
    Expense: Sold:
    $_____   ÷   _____   =   _____._____

10. Total Cost: Per Unit
    (Items 2 and 4 through 9)   _____._____

11. Gross Profit per Unit (Price less Total Cost)   _____._____

12. Overhead: Units Sold:
    $_____   ÷   _____   =   _____._____

13. Profit per Unit (Before Taxes) . . . .   _____._____
    (Item 11 less item 12)

Form P-7: Product Cost and Profit Analysis

COMPANY NO. _____ QUARTER NO. _____

PREPARED BY _____

1. Current Selling Price . . . .   _____._____

2. Per-Unit Production Cost
   e.g., Variable Cost (from printout) . . . .   _____._____

3. Contribution Margin
   (Item 1 − 2) . . . .   _____._____

4. Production   Units
   Engineering   Sold:
   $_____ ÷ _____ = _____._____

5. Inventory   Units
   Expense: Sold:
   $_____ ÷ _____ = _____._____

6. Marketing   Units
   Expense: Sold:
   $_____ ÷ _____ = _____._____

7. R & D   Units
   Expense: Sold:
   $_____ ÷ _____ = _____._____

8. Interest   Units
   Expense: Sold:
   $_____ ÷ _____ = _____._____

9. Depreciation   Units
   Expense: Sold:
   $_____ ÷ _____ = _____._____

10. Total Cost: Per Unit
    (Items 2 and 4 through 9)   _____._____

11. Gross Profit per Unit (Price less Total Cost)   _____._____

12. Overhead: Units Sold:
    $_____ ÷ _____ =   _____._____

13. Profit per Unit (Before Taxes) . . . .   _____._____
    (Item 11 less item 12)

Form P-7: Product Cost and Profit Analysis

COMPANY NO. _____ QUARTER NO. _____

PREPARED BY _____

1. Current Selling Price . . . . _____._____

2. Per-Unit Production Cost
   e.g., Variable Cost (from printout) . . . . _____._____

3. Contribution Margin
   (Item 1 − 2) . . . . _____._____

4. Production   Units
   Engineering   Sold:
   $_____ ÷ _____ = _____._____

5. Inventory   Units
   Expense: Sold:
   $_____ ÷ _____ = _____._____

6. Marketing   Units
   Expense: Sold:
   $_____ ÷ _____ = _____._____

7. R & D   Units
   Expense: Sold:
   $_____ ÷ _____ = _____._____

8. Interest   Units
   Expense: Sold:
   $_____ ÷ _____ = _____._____

9. Depreciation   Units
   Expense: Sold:
   $_____ ÷ _____ = _____._____

10. Total Cost: Per Unit
    (Items 2 and 4 through 9)   _____._____

11. Gross Profit per Unit (Price less Total Cost)   _____._____

12. Overhead: Units Sold:
    $_____ ÷ _____ =   _____._____

13. Profit per Unit (Before Taxes) . . . . _____._____
    (Item 11 less item 12)

Form P-7: Product Cost and Profit Analysis

COMPANY NO. _____ QUARTER NO. _____

PREPARED BY _____

1. Current Selling Price . . . .   _____._____

2. Per-Unit Production Cost
   e.g., Variable Cost (from printout) . . . .   _____._____

3. Contribution Margin
   (Item 1 − 2) . . . .   _____._____

4. Production   Units
   Engineering   Sold:
   $_____   ÷   _____ = _____._____

5. Inventory   Units
   Expense: Sold:
   $_____   ÷   _____ = _____._____

6. Marketing   Units
   Expense: Sold:
   $_____   ÷   _____ = _____._____

7. R & D   Units
   Expense: Sold:
   $_____   ÷   _____ = _____._____

8. Interest   Units
   Expense: Sold:
   $_____   ÷   _____ = _____._____

9. Depreciation   Units
   Expense: Sold:
   $_____   ÷   _____ = _____._____

10. Total Cost: Per Unit
    (Items 2 and 4 through 9)   _____._____

11. Gross Profit per Unit (Price less Total Cost)   _____._____

12. Overhead: Units Sold:
    $_____   ÷   _____ =   _____._____

13. Profit per Unit (Before Taxes) . . . .   _____._____
    (Item 11 less item 12)

Form P-7:   Product Cost and Profit Analysis

COMPANY NO. _____ QUARTER NO. _____

PREPARED BY _____

1. Current Selling Price . . . .   _____ . ____

2. Per-Unit Production Cost
    e.g., Variable Cost (from printout) . . . .   _____ . ____

3. Contribution Margin
    (Item 1 − 2) . . . .   _____ . ____

4. Production   Units
    Engineering   Sold:
    $_____ ÷ _____ = _____ . ____

5. Inventory   Units
    Expense: Sold:
    $_____ ÷ _____ = _____ . ____

6. Marketing   Units
    Expense: Sold:
    $_____ ÷ _____ = _____ . ____

7. R & D   Units
    Expense: Sold:
    $_____ ÷ _____ = _____ . ____

8. Interest   Units
    Expense: Sold:
    $_____ ÷ _____ = _____ . ____

9. Depreciation   Units
    Expense: Sold:
    $_____ ÷ _____ = _____ . ____

10. Total Cost: Per Unit
    (Items 2 and 4 through 9)   _____ . ____

11. Gross Profit per Unit (Price less Total Cost)   _____ . ____

12. Overhead: Units Sold:
    $_____ ÷ _____ =   _____ . ____

13. Profit per Unit (Before Taxes) . . . .   _____ . ____
    (Item 11 less item 12)

Form P-7:   Product Cost and Profit Analysis

COMPANY NO. _____ QUARTER NO. _____

PREPARED BY _____

1. Current Selling Price . . . .   _____._____

2. Per-Unit Production Cost
   e.g., Variable Cost (from printout) . . . .   _____._____

3. Contribution Margin
   (Item 1 – 2) . . . .   _____._____

4. Production   Units
   Engineering   Sold:
   $_____ ÷ _____ = _____.____

5. Inventory   Units
   Expense: Sold:
   $_____ ÷ _____ = _____.____

6. Marketing   Units
   Expense: Sold:
   $_____ ÷ _____ = _____.____

7. R & D   Units
   Expense: Sold:
   $_____ ÷ _____ = _____.____

8. Interest   Units
   Expense: Sold:
   $_____ ÷ _____ = _____.____

9. Depreciation   Units
   Expense: Sold:
   $_____ ÷ _____ = _____.____

10. Total Cost: Per Unit
    (Items 2 and 4 through 9)   _____._____

11. Gross Profit per Unit (Price less Total Cost)   _____._____

12. Overhead: Units Sold:
    $_____ ÷ _____ =   _____._____

13. Profit per Unit (Before Taxes) . . . .   _____._____
    (Item 11 less item 12)

Form P-7:   Product Cost and Profit Analysis

COMPANY NO. _____ QUARTER NO. _____

PREPARED BY _____

1. Current Selling Price . . . .   _____._____

2. Per-Unit Production Cost
    e.g., Variable Cost (from printout) . . . .   _____._____

3. Contribution Margin
    (Item 1 − 2) . . . .   _____._____

4. Production   Units
    Engineering   Sold:
    $_____ ÷ _____ = _____._____

5. Inventory   Units
    Expense: Sold:
    $_____ ÷ _____ = _____._____

6. Marketing   Units
    Expense: Sold:
    $_____ ÷ _____ = _____._____

7. R & D   Units
    Expense: Sold:
    $_____ ÷ _____ = _____._____

8. Interest   Units
    Expense: Sold:
    $_____ ÷ _____ = _____._____

9. Depreciation   Units
    Expense: Sold:
    $_____ ÷ _____ = _____._____

10. Total Cost: Per Unit
    (Items 2 and 4 through 9)   _____._____

11. Gross Profit per Unit (Price less Total Cost)   _____._____

12. Overhead: Units Sold:
    $_____ ÷ _____ =   _____._____

13. Profit per Unit (Before Taxes) . . . .   _____._____
    (Item 11 less item 12)

Form P-7: Product Cost and Profit Analysis

COMPANY NO. _____ QUARTER NO. _____

PREPARED BY _____,

1. Current Selling Price . . . .   _____._____

2. Per-Unit Production Cost
    e.g., Variable Cost (from printout) . . . .   _____._____

3. Contribution Margin
    (Item 1 − 2) . . . .   _____._____

4. Production
    Engineering   Units
    $_____   Sold:
                    ÷ _____ = _____._____

5. Inventory   Units
    Expense: Sold:
    $_____   ÷ _____ = _____._____

6. Marketing   Units
    Expense: Sold:
    $_____   ÷ _____ = _____._____

7. R & D   Units
    Expense: Sold:
    $_____   ÷ _____ = _____._____

8. Interest   Units
    Expense: Sold:
    $_____   ÷ _____ = _____._____

9. Depreciation   Units
    Expense: Sold:
    $_____   ÷ _____ = _____._____

10. Total Cost: Per Unit
    (Items 2 and 4 through 9)   _____._____

11. Gross Profit per Unit (Price less Total Cost)   _____._____

12. Overhead: Units Sold:
    $_____   ÷ _____ =   _____._____

13. Profit per Unit (Before Taxes) . . . .   _____._____
    (Item 11 less item 12)

Form C-8: Cash Flow Analysis

COMPANY NO._____ QUARTER NO. _____

PREPARED BY _____

Cash Outflow

Production Cost:

_____ units @ _____ each $_____

Production Engineering   _____

Inventory Expense   _____

Marketing Expense   _____

Research & Dev. Expense   _____

Other Expense   _____

Interest Expense   _____

Overhead & Fixed Expense   _____

Income Tax (estimated)   _____

Dividends   _____

Total Expenses   _____

Plant Addition and/or
replace depreciation:
_____ units needed @ $40 ea.   _____

Loan Repayment   _____

Total Cash Needed[2]   _____

Cash Inflow

Expected Sales:

_____ units @ _____ each $_____

Common Stock Sold   _____

Bank Loan   _____

Total Funds Available[1]   _____

Less Cash Needed (from
last item in left column)   _____

Ending Cash (estimate)   _____

Note: If Total Funds Available[1] is less than Total Cash Needed,[2] then your firm will need to raise additional capital through either stock sales or a bank loan.

Form C-8:   Cash Flow Analysis

COMPANY NO._____ QUARTER NO. _____

PREPARED BY _____

Cash Outflow

Production Cost:

_____ units @ _____ each $_____

Production Engineering   _____

Inventory Expense   _____

Marketing Expense   _____

Research & Dev. Expense   _____

Other Expense   _____

Interest Expense   _____

Overhead & Fixed Expense   _____

Income Tax (estimated)   _____

Dividends   _____

Total Expenses   _____

Plant Addition and/or
replace depreciation:
_____ units needed @ $40 ea.   _____

Loan Repayment   _____

Total Cash Needed[2]   _____

Cash Inflow

Expected Sales:

_____ units @ _____ each $_____

Common Stock Sold   _____

Bank Loan   _____
          _____

Total Funds Available[1]   _____

Less Cash Needed (from
last item in left column)   _____
          _____

Ending Cash (estimate)   _____

Note: If Total Funds Available[1] is less than Total Cash Needed,[2] then your firm will need to raise additional capital through either stock sales or a bank loan.

Form C-8:   Cash Flow Analysis

COMPANY NO._____ QUARTER NO. _____

PREPARED BY _____

Cash Outflow		*Cash Inflow*	
Production Cost:		Expected Sales:	
_____ units @ _____ each	$_____	_____ units @ _____ each	$_____
Production Engineering	_____	Common Stock Sold	_____
Inventory Expense	_____	Bank Loan	_____
			_____
Marketing Expense	_____	Total Funds Available[1]	_____
Research & Dev. Expense	_____	Less Cash Needed (from last item in left column)	_____
Other Expense	_____		_____
Interest Expense	_____	Ending Cash (estimate)	_____
Overhead & Fixed Expense	_____		
Income Tax (estimated)	_____		
Dividends	_____		
Total Expenses	_____		
Plant Addition and/or replace depreciation: _____ units needed @ $40 ea.	_____		
Loan Repayment	_____		
Total Cash Needed[2]	_____		

Note: If Total Funds Available[1] is less than Total Cash Needed,[2] then your firm will need to raise additional capital through either stock sales or a bank loan.

Form C-8:   Cash Flow Analysis

COMPANY NO._____ QUARTER NO. _____

PREPARED BY _____

Cash Outflow		*Cash Inflow*	
Production Cost:		Expected Sales:	
_____ units @ _____ each	$_____	_____ units @ _____ each	$_____
Production Engineering	_____	Common Stock Sold	_____
Inventory Expense	_____	Bank Loan	_____
			_____
Marketing Expense	_____	Total Funds Available[1]	_____
Research & Dev. Expense	_____	Less Cash Needed (from last item in left column)	_____
Other Expense	_____		_____
Interest Expense	_____	Ending Cash (estimate)	_____
Overhead & Fixed Expense	_____		
Income Tax (estimated)	_____		
Dividends	_____		
Total Expenses	_____		
Plant Addition and/or replace depreciation: _____ units needed @ $40 ea.	_____		
Loan Repayment	_____		
Total Cash Needed[2]	_____		

Note: If Total Funds Available[1] is less than Total Cash Needed,[2] then your firm will need to raise additional capital through either stock sales or a bank loan.

Form C-8: Cash Flow Analysis

COMPANY NO._____ QUARTER NO. _____

PREPARED BY _____

Cash Outflow		*Cash Inflow*	
Production Cost:		Expected Sales:	
_____ units @ _____ each	$_____	_____ units @ _____ each	$_____
Production Engineering	_____	Common Stock Sold	_____
Inventory Expense	_____	Bank Loan	_____
			_____
Marketing Expense	_____	Total Funds Available[1]	_____
Research & Dev. Expense	_____	Less Cash Needed (from last item in left column)	_____
Other Expense	_____		_____
Interest Expense	_____	Ending Cash (estimate)	_____
Overhead & Fixed Expense	_____		
Income Tax (estimated)	_____		
Dividends	_____		
Total Expenses	_____		
Plant Addition and/or replace depreciation: _____ units needed @ $40 ea.	_____		
Loan Repayment	_____		
Total Cash Needed[2]	_____		

Note: If Total Funds Available[1] is less than Total Cash Needed,[2] then your firm will need to raise additional capital through either stock sales or a bank loan.

Form C-8: Cash Flow Analysis

COMPANY NO._____ QUARTER NO. _____

PREPARED BY _____

Cash Outflow		*Cash Inflow*	
Production Cost:		Expected Sales:	
_____ units @ _____ each	$_____	_____ units @ _____ each	$_____
Production Engineering	_____	Common Stock Sold	_____
Inventory Expense	_____	Bank Loan	_____
			_____
Marketing Expense	_____	Total Funds Available[1]	_____
Research & Dev. Expense	_____	Less Cash Needed (from last item in left column)	_____
Other Expense	_____		_____
Interest Expense	_____	Ending Cash (estimate)	_____
Overhead & Fixed Expense	_____		
Income Tax (estimated)	_____		
Dividends	_____		
Total Expenses	_____		
Plant Addition and/or replace depreciation: _____ units needed @ $40 ea.	_____		
Loan Repayment	_____		
Total Cash Needed[2]	_____		

Note: If Total Funds Available[1] is less than Total Cash Needed,[2] then your firm will need to raise additional capital through either stock sales or a bank loan.

Form C-8: Cash Flow Analysis

COMPANY NO._____ QUARTER NO. _____

PREPARED BY _____

Cash Outflow

Production Cost:

_____ units @ _____ each $_____

Production Engineering   _____

Inventory Expense   _____

Marketing Expense   _____

Research & Dev. Expense   _____

Other Expense   _____

Interest Expense   _____

Overhead & Fixed Expense   _____

Income Tax (estimated)   _____

Dividends   _____

Total Expenses   _____

Plant Addition and/or
replace depreciation:
_____ units needed @ $40 ea.   _____

Loan Repayment   _____

Total Cash Needed[2]   _____

Cash Inflow

Expected Sales:

_____ units @ _____ each $_____

Common Stock Sold   _____

Bank Loan   _____

Total Funds Available[1]   _____

Less Cash Needed (from
last item in left column)   _____

Ending Cash (estimate)   _____

Note: If Total Funds Available[1] is less than Total Cash Needed,[2] then your firm will need to raise additional capital through either stock sales or a bank loan.

Form C-8: Cash Flow Analysis

COMPANY NO._____ QUARTER NO. _____

PREPARED BY _____

Cash Outflow		*Cash Inflow*	
Production Cost:		Expected Sales:	
_____ units @ _____ each	$_____	_____ units @ _____ each	$_____
Production Engineering	_____	Common Stock Sold	_____
Inventory Expense	_____	Bank Loan	_____
			_____
Marketing Expense	_____	Total Funds Available[1]	_____
Research & Dev. Expense	_____	Less Cash Needed (from	
Other Expense	_____	last item in left column)	_____
			_____
Interest Expense	_____	Ending Cash (estimate)	_____
Overhead & Fixed Expense	_____		
Income Tax (estimated)	_____		
Dividends	_____		
Total Expenses	_____		
Plant Addition and/or replace depreciation: _____ units needed @ $40 ea.	_____		
Loan Repayment	_____		
Total Cash Needed[2]	_____		

Note: If Total Funds Available[1] is less than Total Cash Needed,[2] then your firm will need to raise additional capital through either stock sales or a bank loan.

Form C-8:   Cash Flow Analysis

COMPANY NO._____ QUARTER NO. _____

PREPARED BY _____

Cash Outflow

Production Cost:

_____ units @ _____ each $_____

Production Engineering   _____

Inventory Expense   _____

Marketing Expense   _____

Research & Dev. Expense   _____

Other Expense   _____

Interest Expense   _____

Overhead & Fixed Expense   _____

Income Tax (estimated)   _____

Dividends   _____

Total Expenses   _____

Plant Addition and/or
replace depreciation:
_____ units needed @ $40 ea.   _____

Loan Repayment   _____

Total Cash Needed[2]   _____

Cash Inflow

Expected Sales:

_____ units @ _____ each $_____

Common Stock Sold   _____

Bank Loan   _____

Total Funds Available[1]   _____

Less Cash Needed (from
last item in left column)   _____

Ending Cash (estimate)   _____

Note: If Total Funds Available[1] is less than Total Cash Needed,[2] then your firm will need to raise additional capital through either stock sales or a bank loan.

© 1984 Houghton Mifflin Company

Form D-9:   Decision Form

QUARTER NO. _____ COMPANY NO. _____

INDUSTRY NO. _____

1. PRICE $____.____

2. MARKETING $_____,000

3. PRODUCTION (IN UNITS)   _____,000

4. PRODUCTION ENGINEERING $_____,000

5. RESEARCH & DEVELOPMENT $_____,000

6. PLANT ADDITION (IN DOLLARS) $_____,000

7. DIVIDENDS PAID $_____,000

8. OTHER EXPENSE $_____,000

9. BANK LOAN OR REPAYMENT $_____,000

10. STOCK SOLD (IN DOLLARS) $_____,000

11. INCIDENT   _____
                                                              _____

VERIFICATION TOTAL[1]   [   ]

* * * * * * * * * * * * * * * * * * * *

[1]NOTE: ADD ALL NUMBERS FROM ITEM 1 THROUGH 11 AND PLACE TOTAL (IN-CLUDING INCIDENT NUMBERS AND ANY DIGITS TO THE RIGHT OF THE DECIMAL) IN THE VERIFICATION BOX. THE VERIFICATION TOTAL SHOULD BE TOTALED ALGEBRAICALLY: NEGATIVE NUMBERS SHOULD BE SUBTRACTED FROM THE TOTAL. THIS IS USED ONLY TO VERIFY THE CORRECTNESS OF THE NUMBERS AS THEY ARE TYPED INTO THE COMPUTER. PLEASE BE SURE YOUR VERIFICATION TOTAL IS CORRECT.

OTHER INSTRUCTIONS: Omit thousands (000) from the decision form. Do *not* use commas. Put a zero (0) in any item not used. A bank loan repayment is indicated by a minus sign (−) preceding the amount to be repaid. Additional plant capacity can be constructed by expending $4,000 for each 100 units desired. (Remember, $4,000 is written as *4* in the decision blank above.)

Form D-9: Decision Form

QUARTER NO. _____ COMPANY NO. _____

INDUSTRY NO. _____

1. PRICE $_____.____

2. MARKETING $_____,000

3. PRODUCTION (IN UNITS) _____,000

4. PRODUCTION ENGINEERING $_____,000

5. RESEARCH & DEVELOPMENT $_____,000

6. PLANT ADDITION (IN DOLLARS) $_____,000

7. DIVIDENDS PAID $_____,000

8. OTHER EXPENSE $_____,000

9. BANK LOAN OR REPAYMENT $_____,000

10. STOCK SOLD (IN DOLLARS) $_____,000

11. INCIDENT _____
_____

VERIFICATION TOTAL[1]

* *

[1]NOTE: ADD ALL NUMBERS FROM ITEM 1 THROUGH 11 AND PLACE TOTAL (IN-CLUDING INCIDENT NUMBERS AND ANY DIGITS TO THE RIGHT OF THE DECIMAL) IN THE VERIFICATION BOX. THE VERIFICATION TOTAL SHOULD BE TOTALED ALGEBRAICALLY: NEGATIVE NUMBERS SHOULD BE SUBTRACTED FROM THE TOTAL. THIS IS USED ONLY TO VERIFY THE CORRECTNESS OF THE NUMBERS AS THEY ARE TYPED INTO THE COMPUTER. PLEASE BE SURE YOUR VERIFICATION TOTAL IS CORRECT.

OTHER INSTRUCTIONS: Omit thousands (000) from the decision form. Do *not* use commas. Put a zero (0) in any item not used. A bank loan repayment is indicated by a minus sign (−) preceding the amount to be repaid. Additional plant capacity can be con-structed by expending $4,000 for each 100 units desired. (Remember, $4,000 is written as *4* in the decision blank above.)

Form D-9:   Decision Form

QUARTER NO. _____ COMPANY NO. _____

INDUSTRY NO. _____

1. PRICE $_____.____

2. MARKETING $_____,000

3. PRODUCTION (IN UNITS) _____,000

4. PRODUCTION ENGINEERING $_____,000

5. RESEARCH & DEVELOPMENT $_____,000

6. PLANT ADDITION (IN DOLLARS) $_____,000

7. DIVIDENDS PAID $_____,000

8. OTHER EXPENSE $_____,000

9. BANK LOAN OR REPAYMENT $_____,000

10. STOCK SOLD (IN DOLLARS) $_____,000

11. INCIDENT _____

VERIFICATION TOTAL[1]

* * * * * * * * * * * * * * * * * * * *

[1]NOTE: ADD ALL NUMBERS FROM ITEM 1 THROUGH 11 AND PLACE TOTAL (IN-CLUDING INCIDENT NUMBERS AND ANY DIGITS TO THE RIGHT OF THE DECIMAL) IN THE VERIFICATION BOX. THE VERIFICATION TOTAL SHOULD BE TOTALED ALGEBRAICALLY: NEGATIVE NUMBERS SHOULD BE SUBTRACTED FROM THE TOTAL. THIS IS USED ONLY TO VERIFY THE CORRECTNESS OF THE NUMBERS AS THEY ARE TYPED INTO THE COMPUTER. PLEASE BE SURE YOUR VERIFICATION TOTAL IS CORRECT.

OTHER INSTRUCTIONS: Omit thousands (000) from the decision form. Do *not* use commas. Put a zero (0) in any item not used. A bank loan repayment is indicated by a minus sign (−) preceding the amount to be repaid. Additional plant capacity can be constructed by expending $4,000 for each 100 units desired. (Remember, $4,000 is written as *4* in the decision blank above.)

Form D-9: Decision Form

QUARTER NO. _____ COMPANY NO. _____

INDUSTRY NO. _____

1. PRICE $_____.____

2. MARKETING $_____,000

3. PRODUCTION (IN UNITS)   _____,000

4. PRODUCTION ENGINEERING $_____,000

5. RESEARCH & DEVELOPMENT $_____,000

6. PLANT ADDITION (IN DOLLARS) $_____,000

7. DIVIDENDS PAID $_____,000

8. OTHER EXPENSE $_____,000

9. BANK LOAN OR REPAYMENT $_____,000

10. STOCK SOLD (IN DOLLARS) $_____,000

11. INCIDENT   _____
                                              _____

VERIFICATION TOTAL[1]   ┌──────────────┐
                                           └──────────────┘

****

[1]NOTE: ADD ALL NUMBERS FROM ITEM 1 THROUGH 11 AND PLACE TOTAL (IN-CLUDING INCIDENT NUMBERS AND ANY DIGITS TO THE RIGHT OF THE DECIMAL) IN THE VERIFICATION BOX. THE VERIFICATION TOTAL SHOULD BE TOTALED ALGEBRAICALLY: NEGATIVE NUMBERS SHOULD BE SUBTRACTED FROM THE TOTAL. THIS IS USED ONLY TO VERIFY THE CORRECTNESS OF THE NUMBERS AS THEY ARE TYPED INTO THE COMPUTER. PLEASE BE SURE YOUR VERIFICATION TOTAL IS CORRECT.

OTHER INSTRUCTIONS: Omit thousands (000) from the decision form. Do *not* use commas. Put a zero (0) in any item not used. A bank loan repayment is indicated by a minus sign (−) preceding the amount to be repaid. Additional plant capacity can be constructed by expending $4,000 for each 100 units desired. (Remember, $4,000 is written as *4* in the decision blank above.)

Form D-9:   Decision Form

QUARTER NO. _____ COMPANY NO. _____

INDUSTRY NO. _____

1. PRICE $_____._____

2. MARKETING $_____,000

3. PRODUCTION (IN UNITS)   _____,000

4. PRODUCTION ENGINEERING $_____,000

5. RESEARCH & DEVELOPMENT $_____,000

6. PLANT ADDITION (IN DOLLARS) $_____,000

7. DIVIDENDS PAID $_____,000

8. OTHER EXPENSE $_____,000

9. BANK LOAN OR REPAYMENT $_____,000

10. STOCK SOLD (IN DOLLARS) $_____,000

11. INCIDENT   _____

VERIFICATION TOTAL[1]

* * * * * * * * * * * * * * * * * * * *

[1]NOTE: ADD ALL NUMBERS FROM ITEM 1 THROUGH 11 AND PLACE TOTAL (IN-CLUDING INCIDENT NUMBERS AND ANY DIGITS TO THE RIGHT OF THE DECIMAL) IN THE VERIFICATION BOX. THE VERIFICATION TOTAL SHOULD BE TOTALED ALGEBRAICALLY: NEGATIVE NUMBERS SHOULD BE SUBTRACTED FROM THE TOTAL. THIS IS USED ONLY TO VERIFY THE CORRECTNESS OF THE NUMBERS AS THEY ARE TYPED INTO THE COMPUTER. PLEASE BE SURE YOUR VERIFICATION TOTAL IS CORRECT.

OTHER INSTRUCTIONS: Omit thousands (000) from the decision form. Do *not* use commas. Put a zero (0) in any item not used. A bank loan repayment is indicated by a minus sign (−) preceding the amount to be repaid. Additional plant capacity can be constructed by expending $4,000 for each 100 units desired. (Remember, $4,000 is written as *4* in the decision blank above.)

Form D-9: Decision Form

QUARTER NO. _____ COMPANY NO. _____

INDUSTRY NO. _____

1. PRICE $_____.____

2. MARKETING $_____,000

3. PRODUCTION (IN UNITS)   _____,000

4. PRODUCTION ENGINEERING $_____,000

5. RESEARCH & DEVELOPMENT $_____,000

6. PLANT ADDITION (IN DOLLARS) $_____,000

7. DIVIDENDS PAID $_____,000

8. OTHER EXPENSE $_____,000

9. BANK LOAN OR REPAYMENT $_____,000

10. STOCK SOLD (IN DOLLARS) $_____,000

11. INCIDENT   _____
                                                      _____

VERIFICATION TOTAL[1]   [_____]

* * * * * * * * * * * * * * * * * * * *

[1]NOTE: ADD ALL NUMBERS FROM ITEM 1 THROUGH 11 AND PLACE TOTAL (IN-CLUDING INCIDENT NUMBERS AND ANY DIGITS TO THE RIGHT OF THE DECIMAL) IN THE VERIFICATION BOX. THE VERIFICATION TOTAL SHOULD BE TOTALED ALGEBRAICALLY: NEGATIVE NUMBERS SHOULD BE SUBTRACTED FROM THE TOTAL. THIS IS USED ONLY TO VERIFY THE CORRECTNESS OF THE NUMBERS AS THEY ARE TYPED INTO THE COMPUTER. PLEASE BE SURE YOUR VERIFICATION TOTAL IS CORRECT.

OTHER INSTRUCTIONS: Omit thousands (000) from the decision form. Do *not* use commas. Put a zero (0) in any item not used. A bank loan repayment is indicated by a minus sign (−) preceding the amount to be repaid. Additional plant capacity can be constructed by expending $4,000 for each 100 units desired. (Remember, $4,000 is written as *4* in the decision blank above.)

Form D-9:   Decision Form

QUARTER NO. _____ COMPANY NO. _____

INDUSTRY NO. _____

1. PRICE $_____ . _____

2. MARKETING $_____ ,000

3. PRODUCTION (IN UNITS)   _____ ,000

4. PRODUCTION ENGINEERING $_____ ,000

5. RESEARCH & DEVELOPMENT $_____ ,000

6. PLANT ADDITION (IN DOLLARS) $_____ ,000

7. DIVIDENDS PAID $_____ ,000

8. OTHER EXPENSE $_____ ,000

9. BANK LOAN OR REPAYMENT $_____ ,000

10. STOCK SOLD (IN DOLLARS) $_____ ,000

11. INCIDENT   _____

VERIFICATION TOTAL[1]

* * * * * * * * * * * * * * * * * * * *

[1]NOTE: ADD ALL NUMBERS FROM ITEM 1 THROUGH 11 AND PLACE TOTAL (IN-
CLUDING INCIDENT NUMBERS AND ANY DIGITS TO THE RIGHT OF THE DECIMAL)
IN THE VERIFICATION BOX. THE VERIFICATION TOTAL SHOULD BE TOTALED
ALGEBRAICALLY: NEGATIVE NUMBERS SHOULD BE SUBTRACTED FROM THE
TOTAL. THIS IS USED ONLY TO VERIFY THE CORRECTNESS OF THE NUMBERS AS
THEY ARE TYPED INTO THE COMPUTER. PLEASE BE SURE YOUR VERIFICATION
TOTAL IS CORRECT.

OTHER INSTRUCTIONS: Omit thousands (000) from the decision form. Do *not* use
commas. Put a zero (0) in any item not used. A bank loan repayment is indicated by a
minus sign (−) preceding the amount to be repaid. Additional plant capacity can be constructed by expending $4,000 for each 100 units desired. (Remember, $4,000 is written
as *4* in the decision blank above.)

© 1984 Houghton Mifflin Company

Form D-9: Decision Form

QUARTER NO. _____ COMPANY NO. _____

INDUSTRY NO. _____

1. PRICE $_____.____

2. MARKETING $_____,000

3. PRODUCTION (IN UNITS)   _____,000

4. PRODUCTION ENGINEERING $_____,000

5. RESEARCH & DEVELOPMENT $_____,000

6. PLANT ADDITION (IN DOLLARS) $_____,000

7. DIVIDENDS PAID $_____,000

8. OTHER EXPENSE $_____,000

9. BANK LOAN OR REPAYMENT $_____,000

10. STOCK SOLD (IN DOLLARS) $_____,000

11. INCIDENT   _____

VERIFICATION TOTAL[1]

* * * * * * * * * * * * * * * * * * * *

[1]NOTE: ADD ALL NUMBERS FROM ITEM 1 THROUGH 11 AND PLACE TOTAL (IN-CLUDING INCIDENT NUMBERS AND ANY DIGITS TO THE RIGHT OF THE DECIMAL) IN THE VERIFICATION BOX. THE VERIFICATION TOTAL SHOULD BE TOTALED ALGEBRAICALLY: NEGATIVE NUMBERS SHOULD BE SUBTRACTED FROM THE TOTAL. THIS IS USED ONLY TO VERIFY THE CORRECTNESS OF THE NUMBERS AS THEY ARE TYPED INTO THE COMPUTER. PLEASE BE SURE YOUR VERIFICATION TOTAL IS CORRECT.

OTHER INSTRUCTIONS: Omit thousands (000) from the decision form. Do *not* use commas. Put a zero (0) in any item not used. A bank loan repayment is indicated by a minus sign (−) preceding the amount to be repaid. Additional plant capacity can be constructed by expending $4,000 for each 100 units desired. (Remember, $4,000 is written as *4* in the decision blank above.)

Form D-9: Decision Form

QUARTER NO. _____ COMPANY NO. _____

INDUSTRY NO. _____

1. PRICE $_____.____

2. MARKETING $_____,000

3. PRODUCTION (IN UNITS)   _____,000

4. PRODUCTION ENGINEERING $_____,000

5. RESEARCH & DEVELOPMENT $_____,000

6. PLANT ADDITION (IN DOLLARS) $_____,000

7. DIVIDENDS PAID $_____,000

8. OTHER EXPENSE $_____,000

9. BANK LOAN OR REPAYMENT $_____,000

10. STOCK SOLD (IN DOLLARS) $_____,000

11. INCIDENT   _____

VERIFICATION TOTAL[1]

* * * * * * * * * * * * * * * * * * * *

[1]NOTE: ADD ALL NUMBERS FROM ITEM 1 THROUGH 11 AND PLACE TOTAL (IN-CLUDING INCIDENT NUMBERS AND ANY DIGITS TO THE RIGHT OF THE DECIMAL) IN THE VERIFICATION BOX. THE VERIFICATION TOTAL SHOULD BE TOTALED ALGEBRAICALLY: NEGATIVE NUMBERS SHOULD BE SUBTRACTED FROM THE TOTAL. THIS IS USED ONLY TO VERIFY THE CORRECTNESS OF THE NUMBERS AS THEY ARE TYPED INTO THE COMPUTER. PLEASE BE SURE YOUR VERIFICATION TOTAL IS CORRECT.

OTHER INSTRUCTIONS: Omit thousands (000) from the decision form. Do *not* use commas. Put a zero (0) in any item not used. A bank loan repayment is indicated by a minus sign (−) preceding the amount to be repaid. Additional plant capacity can be constructed by expending $4,000 for each 100 units desired. (Remember, $4,000 is written as *4* in the decision blank above.)

Form D-9:   Decision Form

QUARTER NO. _____ COMPANY NO. _____

INDUSTRY NO. _____

1. PRICE $____.____

2. MARKETING $_____,000

3. PRODUCTION (IN UNITS)   _____,000

4. PRODUCTION ENGINEERING $_____,000

5. RESEARCH & DEVELOPMENT $_____,000

6. PLANT ADDITION (IN DOLLARS) $_____,000

7. DIVIDENDS PAID $_____,000

8. OTHER EXPENSE $_____,000

9. BANK LOAN OR REPAYMENT $_____,000

10. STOCK SOLD (IN DOLLARS) $_____,000

11. INCIDENT   _____
                                                       _____

VERIFICATION TOTAL[1]   [_____]

* * * * * * * * * * * * * * * * * * * *

[1]NOTE: ADD ALL NUMBERS FROM ITEM 1 THROUGH 11 AND PLACE TOTAL (IN-CLUDING INCIDENT NUMBERS AND ANY DIGITS TO THE RIGHT OF THE DECIMAL) IN THE VERIFICATION BOX. THE VERIFICATION TOTAL SHOULD BE TOTALED ALGEBRAICALLY: NEGATIVE NUMBERS SHOULD BE SUBTRACTED FROM THE TOTAL. THIS IS USED ONLY TO VERIFY THE CORRECTNESS OF THE NUMBERS AS THEY ARE TYPED INTO THE COMPUTER. PLEASE BE SURE YOUR VERIFICATION TOTAL IS CORRECT.

OTHER INSTRUCTIONS: Omit thousands (000) from the decision form. Do *not* use commas. Put a zero (0) in any item not used. A bank loan repayment is indicated by a minus sign (−) preceding the amount to be repaid. Additional plant capacity can be constructed by expending $4,000 for each 100 units desired. (Remember, $4,000 is written as *4* in the decision blank above.)

Form D-9:   Decision Form

QUARTER NO. _____ COMPANY NO. _____

INDUSTRY NO. _____

1. PRICE $_____.____

2. MARKETING $_____,000

3. PRODUCTION (IN UNITS)   _____,000

4. PRODUCTION ENGINEERING $_____,000

5. RESEARCH & DEVELOPMENT $_____,000

6. PLANT ADDITION (IN DOLLARS) $_____,000

7. DIVIDENDS PAID $_____,000

8. OTHER EXPENSE $_____,000

9. BANK LOAN OR REPAYMENT $_____,000

10. STOCK SOLD (IN DOLLARS) $_____,000

11. INCIDENT   _____

VERIFICATION TOTAL[1]

* * * * * * * * * * * * * * * * * * * *

[1]NOTE: ADD ALL NUMBERS FROM ITEM 1 THROUGH 11 AND PLACE TOTAL (IN-CLUDING INCIDENT NUMBERS AND ANY DIGITS TO THE RIGHT OF THE DECIMAL) IN THE VERIFICATION BOX. THE VERIFICATION TOTAL SHOULD BE TOTALED ALGEBRAICALLY: NEGATIVE NUMBERS SHOULD BE SUBTRACTED FROM THE TOTAL. THIS IS USED ONLY TO VERIFY THE CORRECTNESS OF THE NUMBERS AS THEY ARE TYPED INTO THE COMPUTER. PLEASE BE SURE YOUR VERIFICATION TOTAL IS CORRECT.

OTHER INSTRUCTIONS: Omit thousands (000) from the decision form. Do *not* use commas. Put a zero (0) in any item not used. A bank loan repayment is indicated by a minus sign (−) preceding the amount to be repaid. Additional plant capacity can be constructed by expending $4,000 for each 100 units desired. (Remember, $4,000 is written as *4* in the decision blank above.)

Form D-9: Decision Form

QUARTER NO. _____ COMPANY NO. _____

INDUSTRY NO. _____

1. PRICE $_____._____

2. MARKETING $_____,000

3. PRODUCTION (IN UNITS)   _____,000

4. PRODUCTION ENGINEERING $_____,000

5. RESEARCH & DEVELOPMENT $_____,000

6. PLANT ADDITION (IN DOLLARS) $_____,000

7. DIVIDENDS PAID $_____,000

8. OTHER EXPENSE $_____,000

9. BANK LOAN OR REPAYMENT $_____,000

10. STOCK SOLD (IN DOLLARS) $_____,000

11. INCIDENT   _____
                                                   _____

VERIFICATION TOTAL[1]

* * * * * * * * * * * * * * * * * * * *

[1]NOTE: ADD ALL NUMBERS FROM ITEM 1 THROUGH 11 AND PLACE TOTAL (IN-CLUDING INCIDENT NUMBERS AND ANY DIGITS TO THE RIGHT OF THE DECIMAL) IN THE VERIFICATION BOX. THE VERIFICATION TOTAL SHOULD BE TOTALED ALGEBRAICALLY: NEGATIVE NUMBERS SHOULD BE SUBTRACTED FROM THE TOTAL. THIS IS USED ONLY TO VERIFY THE CORRECTNESS OF THE NUMBERS AS THEY ARE TYPED INTO THE COMPUTER. PLEASE BE SURE YOUR VERIFICATION TOTAL IS CORRECT.

OTHER INSTRUCTIONS: Omit thousands (000) from the decision form. Do *not* use commas. Put a zero (0) in any item not used. A bank loan repayment is indicated by a minus sign (−) preceding the amount to be repaid. Additional plant capacity can be constructed by expending $4,000 for each 100 units desired. (Remember, $4,000 is written as *4* in the decision blank above.)

© 1984 Houghton Mifflin Company